Syrian Foreign Policy
and the United States

St Andrews Papers
on Contemporary Syria

SERIES EDITOR, RAYMOND HINNEBUSCH

Changing Regime Discourse and Reform in Syria
Aurora Sottimano and Kjetil Selvik

The State and the Political Economy of Reform in Syria
Raymond Hinnebusch and Soren Schmidt

Syria and the Euro-Mediterranean Relationship
Jörg Michael Dostal and Anja Zorob

Syrian Foreign Policy and the United States:
From Bush to Obama
Raymond Hinnebusch, Marwan J. Kabalan,
Bassma Kodmani, and David Lesch

Syrian Foreign Trade and Economic Reform
Samer Abboud and Salam Said

Syria's Economy and the Transition Paradigm
Samer Abboud and Ferdinand Arslanian

Syrian Foreign Policy and the United States

From Bush to Obama

Raymond Hinnebusch, Marwan J. Kabalan,
Bassma Kodmani, David Lesch

University of St Andrews Centre for Syrian Studies

© 2010 by the University of St Andrews Centre for Syrian Studies

Published by the University of St Andrews Centre for Syrian Studies
School of International Relations
Fife, Scotland
UK

Distributed throughout the world by
Lynne Rienner Publishers, Inc.
1800 30th Street
Boulder, CO 80301
USA
www.rienner.com

British Library Cataloguing-in-Publication Data.
A catalogue record for this book is available from the British Library.

Printed and bound in the United States of America

ISBN: 978-0-9559687-5-4

Contents

Foreword
Raymond Hinnebusch

These four analyses look at Syrian foreign policy, and particularly the ups and downs in Syria's relationship with the US since Bashar al-Asad and George W. Bush nearly simultaneously came to power. One of the most striking and puzzling aspects of this relationship is why a Syrian leader keen to improve relations with the West was soon the object of a concerted attempt to demonize and isolate him. Arguably this had more to do with American politics than with Syria, and had Kerry won the 2000 US election US-Syrian relations would almost certainly have taken a much different tangent and the history of the Middle East would have turned out very differently.

The focus of the analyses is, however, on what makes Syria tick and how this explains its strategies in dealing with the hostile, aggressive and powerful US under Bush. The analysis by Hinnebusch looks particularly at the continuities from the Hafiz period, showing how Syria was, in the late nineties, on course for a peace settlement with Israel under US auspices. The failure of the peace negotiations set entrain a series of moves and countermoves that contributed to a crisis in Syrian-US relations, with Iraq and Lebanon the foci of their clashing agendas. The article finishes with a look at the fresh start between the two states at the beginning of the Obama administration. Marwan Kabalan focuses on the link between Syrian domestic and foreign policy: foreign policy is used as much to protect regime survival at home as it is to ward off strategic threats from external enemies. Conversely, Syria's external environment affects the prospects of reform at home; one obvious casualty of the threats mounted by Washington to the Syrian regime was its cautious early political relaxation. David Lesch focuses particularly on how the current president, Bashar al-Asad, sees the world and how he managed to survive the hostility of the world hegemon, learning by his mistakes, while consolidating his position at home. He stresses the extent to which Syria's role, whether problem-maker or problem-solver, depends in great part on whether the US learns to respect its vital interests. Finally, Bassma Kodmani looks at how Bashar has apparently outlasted the campaign to isolate Syria and looks at Bashar's choices and likely strategies in his new, seemingly less threatening, environment.

1

Syria under Bashar:
Between Economic Reform and
Nationalist Realpolitik

Raymond Hinnebusch

On Bashar al-Asad's accession to the presidency in June 2000, Syria was at a crossroads. Its new leader's priority was economic reform, which dictated a Westward foreign policy alignment and depended on a benign international environment. Only six months later, and fatefully for Bashar, George W. Bush was elected President of the US, bringing to power elements determined to impose US hegemony in the Middle East and deeply hostile to Arab nationalism and to Syria. Given the unmatched power and ambition of the US hegemon, which was soon to be on Syria's Iraqi doorstep, and the dependence of Bashar's reform program on integration into Western markets, Syria had powerful security and economic reasons to bandwagon with the US, as all the other Arab states did. Instead, however, it balanced against US power. That it did not bandwagon is ultimately attributable to its distinctive Arab nationalist identity and the accompanying regional role that had been institutionalized in the Ba'thist state, especially under Hafiz al-Asad. That this made the difference is evident from the quite different response of Jordan's King Abdallah who faced similar pressures, but, having constructed a "Jordan first" identity, chose to bandwagon with Washington.[1] Hafiz had not only left a role to his son, but also a tradition of realpolitik that came out of years of experience coping with Syria's many more powerful enemies; it was this tradition that arguably allowed Bashar to survive: when Bush left office in the US he was still president of Syria.

It was not immediately evident when Bashar came to power that the international atmosphere for Syrian reform would sour so rapidly. Indeed, Bashar initially receive a positive welcome from most foreign governments and quickly moved to improve Syria's relations with most of its neighbours, notably Iraq and Turkey, while launching a strategic opening to Europe. What would not have been predicted in 2000 is the way he was soon demonized in various Western circles. A series of external events, notably the breakdown of the peace process, the Iraq war, which Syria opposed, and the assassination of Lebanese ex-Prime minister Rafiq al-Hariri, for which it was blamed, all contributed to precipitating a period of unrelenting US hostility. Under extreme pressure, Syria's Arab nationalist identity was aroused, the regime's old Machiavellian foreign policy instincts revived and the domestic reform agenda was constrained. In spite of this, Syria continued to seek inclusion in the world order, albeit in a way that preserved its identity and interests. A revived strategy of power-balancing against threats to its vital interests from Israel and the US was paralleled by a continuing economic liberalization strategy through which Syria sought to diversify its economic dependencies and acquire the economic resources needed to sustain the regime. This dual strategy appeared to allow Syria to survive the Bush years with limited damage to its interests; the inauguration of the Obama administration posed the prospects that US-Syrian relations might be mended and the environment for domestic economic reform much improved.

Bashar's Foreign Policy Inheritance

Certain relatively durable determinants have conditioned the behaviour of Syrian leaders and Bashar cannot escape this influence, especially as much of it is an inheritance from his father.

First, Syria is imbued with a powerful sense of grievance from the forced partition of historic Syria (*bilad al-sham*) by Western imperialism and the creation of Israel on the territory of geographic southern Syria. Radical Arab nationalism, the dominant identity of the country and ideology of the ruling Ba'th party, is a direct consequence of this experience. Syria's Arab nationalist identity, leading it to support Palestinian *fedayeen* operations against Israel, was a key factor in provoking the 1967 Arab-Israeli war in which Israel captured Syria's Golan Heights. Since then, all Syrian foreign policy behaviour has revolved around the recovery of the Golan. This is a matter of national honour and regime legitimacy.

Equally important for understanding Syria is its pervasive sense of insecurity. It is a small state surrounded by several stronger powers that, at one time or another, have been a threat. Historically its borders have been violated, most recently by both Israel and the US. It faces a great military imbalance, in respect to Israel, and is now sandwiched between Israel in the West and the US in the East (Iraq). As such, Syria continues to perceive a threat from what it takes to be Western imperialism, a view that has been repeatedly reinforced, particularly since the rise of the George W. Bush administration (2000-2008). Syria currently sees the West's policies as replete with double standards. International law is selectively enforced; thus, Syria's chemical deterrent force has been targeted by the West while Israel's nuclear one is accepted. The Iraq war showed how the strong "take the law into their own hands." For Syrians, it is a Machiavellian world where a state's interests are respected only if it has the power to defend them. Hence, great power-engineered demands, advanced in the name of the 'international community,' enjoy no normative legitimacy in Syria. Indeed, Damascus consistently evades the dictates of great powers and those who want something from Syria have to negotiate for it.

Given its threatening environment, Syria's grievances and ambitions have had to be tempered by the reality of its vulnerabilities and weaknesses. Hafiz al-Asad was the first Syrian leader to systematically bridge the gap between Syrian goals and means.[2] On the one hand, he scaled down and replaced Syria's formerly revisionist aim of liberating Palestine with the more realist goals of recovering the Golan and creation of a Palestinian state in the West Bank and Gaza. On the other hand, steadily expanding Syrian military power resulted in a mutual deterrence that relatively stabilized the Syrian-Israeli military confrontation.[3] Syrian-Israeli rivalry was thereby largely diverted into political struggle over the conditions of a peace settlement. In these struggles, Syria's deterrent meant that Asad did not have to bargain from weakness and could apply limited military pressure on Israel in southern Lebanon (via Hizbullah) at reasonable risk.

Second, Hafiz realized, by contrast to his radical predecessors, that Syria could not do without alliances and he assiduously diversified them, relying for a period on Egypt and Saudi Arabia, later on Iran, while balancing close alignment with the USSR, crucial for protection in a predatory world, with a readiness to engage with American diplomacy over a peace settlement. Additionally, because Syria's slim economic base and feeble tax extraction capability could not sustain its enormous military burden, Hafiz used external alliances to access enormous levels of external aid and loans by virtue of Syria's front line status against Israel, largely from the USSR and Arab oil producing states, in order to fill the resultant permanent resource gap. The national-security state Hafiz built greatly enhanced Syria's military security but ultimately helped enervate its weak economic base.

Hafiz was also acutely aware, at least after Syria failed to recover the Golan in the October 1973 war, that this aim, as well as an acceptable resolution of the Palestine issue, made negotiation of a peace settlement with Israel unavoidable. He believed, however, that successful negotiations depended on a sufficient balance of power; if it was too unfavourable, Syria had to be patient and wait until it shifted, while taking advantage of every opportunity to contribute to such a shift. Syria, he believed, should never negotiate from weakness and unless it had bargaining "cards." Effective bargaining might require the use of asymmetric warfare to give the stronger Israeli opponent an incentive to negotiate an acceptable deal; this was best pursued via proxies and not from Syria territory (hence Lebanon became the arena of struggle) and required a military deterrent so that the enemy did not bring his full retaliatory superiority to bear on Syria. Aware, too, that only the US could broker a negotiated settlement, Syria constantly sought to demonstrate to the US that it could advance US objectives, presumed to be regional stability, if its interests were accommodated and if not that it could also block US plans—such as separate peace agreements excluding Syria. Insofar as the US wants a peace settlement in the region, it cannot avoid dealing with Syria, for as Henry Kissinger famously said, the Arabs cannot make war without Egypt or make peace without Syria.

Bashar al-Asad attempted to alter this approach, preferring dialogue to confrontation and deploying a conciliatory and more reasonable personal discourse. However, rising external threats forced him to fall back on his father's modus operendi.

Political Economy Determinants

Just as much a threat to regime survival as external enemies was the vulnerability of the Syrian economy. Bashar al-Asad's reform program was a continuation and deepening of economic liberalization begun under Hafiz that originated in the exhaustion of import substitute industrialization and the statist-populist model from at least the eighties. This was exacerbated by the decline of Arab aid from the 1980s, but interspersed with recoveries when new resources, mostly rent from Syria's own petroleum exports, were accessed. At the end of the 1990s, however, stagnant growth, combined with a burgeoning population resulted in unemployment rates reputedly reaching 20%. These problems threatened to deepen as revenues from oil exports inexorably declined, posing the prospect of a fiscal crisis in the medium term. In the short term, the regime had accumulated considerable reserves in foreign currency to buffer it against emergencies and ease the stress of transition to a market economy. Over the long term, a consensus emerged that, given the stagnation of the public sector, economic survival required a sustained takeoff of private investment which, in turn, depended on Syria's integration into and conformity with the standards of the global market and an accompanying Westcentric foreign policy.

There were, however, formidable obstacles to deepening Syria's economic liberalization, including the rent seeking behaviour of the emergent new crony capitalists around the regime, the "social contract" under which regime legitimacy is contingent on public provision of subsidized food and fuel, state jobs and farm support prices, and the need of the regime to dispense patronage to keep core elites loyal. Moreover, private investment, particularly in long-term productive enterprise, was deterred by bureaucratic obstacles, lack of rule of law, and the regional insecurity generated by interminable regional conflicts. Ironically, just as Bashar launched his reform initiative, regional conflicts substantially worsened. More than that, integration into the Western market had to be reconciled with Syria's Arab nationalist identity and this was impossible as long as the conflict with Israel and Western "imperialism" continued and, indeed, dramatically deepened after 2002.

The failure of the peace negotiations with Israel in 2000 was the first external factor that had important negative consequences for reform prospects; at the end of the nineties, in the expectation of imminent peace, Hafiz, with Bashar as his chief lieutenant, was preparing or initiating major liberalizing and anti-corruption reforms needed to take advantage of a hoped-for major influx of (mostly Arab and expatriate) investment. However, with the failure of the peace process, Bashar's regime had to look elsewhere for resources and found them in an opening to Iraq, hitherto a bitter rival but which was now seeking Syrian co-operation in evading UN sanctions by re-opening the closed pipeline between the two states. Re-export of Iraqi oil sold to Syria at subsidized prices provided a billion dollar yearly windfall to the treasury.

When this lifeline was shut down by the US invasion of Iraq, accompanied by a major and burdensome influx of Iraqi refugees into Syria, the regime actually *accelerated* its economic liberalization in a bid to get a cut of the wealth accruing to the Gulf Arab oil producers from the new post-war oil price boom. In spite of a fraught regional and international environment, Syria did enjoy an influx of Arab investment in the mid-2000s that stabilized the economy and fuelled the crony-capitalist network supportive of the regime. At the same time, however, Syria's determination to hold onto "cards" needed in the struggle with

Israel, manifest in its role in Lebanon and its support of Hizbullah, soured political relations not only with the US, but also for a time with Europe and Saudi Arabia, key economic partners. Very much in doubt also was how far Syria's integration into the world market was compatible with a foreign policy that brought recurrent conflict with the US hegemon; American sanctions worked to economically isolate Syria and Washington pressured Europe to obstruct Syria's bid for an economic association agreement. As a result, Syria shifted its economic relations eastward to Russia, Asia and especially toward China but this could not wholly substitute for relations with the West.

Post-Hafiz Leadership: Bashar's Reformist Project

While it is now taken for granted, Bashar's succession and consolidation of power, without jeopardizing Syria's hard-won stability, was not self-evident to observers in 2000. When Hafiz died, the establishment, fearful of instability, settled on Bashar as its choice: as an Asad, he reassured the Alawis; would not likely betray his father's heritage (not being a Sadat); and he was not seen as a threat to them. Yet he was popular, being seen as uncorrupted and a modernizer, with the public, especially the younger generation.[4] Indeed, Bashar's succession evoked great expectations that generational change in leadership would be a watershed for Syria. When taking office, he spoke of the need to improve and modernize the economy, education and the administration. He also raised expectations of political change by emphasizing 'democratic thinking' and 'the principle of accepting the opinion of the other'.[5] Hence, he represented both continuity and change.

Yet, initially lacking a personal power base and inheriting a state constructed by his predecessor meant he had to share power with several power centres that surrounded the presidency—the party politburo, the cabinet, the army high command and the security forces—all initially dominated by the old guard of his father's close colleagues. He also inherited an experienced foreign policy team from his father, headed by Vice President Khaddam and Foreign Minister Farouk al-Sharaa, that imparted continuity to foreign policy. However, Bashar did soon establish himself as "the prime decision maker" and his reform team became the dominant tendency in the regime.[6] Through the extensive legal powers of his office, he engineered the replacement of the old guard as it reached retirement age with appointees beholden to himself. This process of power concentration was crowned at the 2005 Ba'th party 10th Regional conference by the resignation of Khaddam, the senior old guardist, and some half dozen other top Ba'th party officials.

Aware of the flaws in the Syrian economic model and familiar with the West, Bashar was a reformer at heart, despite the slow pace of actual change. Ba'thist ideology ceased to govern Syria's economic policy but Bashar lacked an elaborate blueprint to substitute for it.[7] The Chinese model of spreading the private sector and the market while retaining a reformed public sector was in principle embraced but it provided only the roughest of guides and reform proceeded piecemeal, by trial and error, and constrained by the need for a consensus within an elite divided over how far and how fast to go.[8] Reform had to be incremental, initially to avoid arousing enemies before Bashar had built up his own reformist faction and thereafter to avoid unleashing social instability.

Bashar's project can be understood as "modernising authoritarianism," making the system work better so that it could survive and deliver development.[9] The first priority was to renew cadres and leadership personnel and he engineered, within three years of succession, a renovation of the political elite, with a turnover of 60% in top offices, thereby transferring power to a new generation.[10] His priorities were reflected in those he recruited to ministerial office, most of whom were technocrats with advanced Western degrees in economics or engineering and favouring integration into the world economy.[11] His reforms included restricting the interference of the party and security forces in economic administration, creating the legal framework for a more market oriented economy, the opening of private banks and insurance companies, trade and foreign exchange liberalization, and internet start up. But he made no direct assault on the new class of "crony capitalists,"—the rent-seeking alliances of Alawi political brokers (now led by his own mother's family, the Makhloufs) and the regime-supportive Sunni bourgeoisie--whose corrupt stranglehold on the economy deterred productive investment; he hoped, instead, to use international economic agreements, notably the Euro-Mediterranean partnership, to force an opening of the economy that would require them to become competitive capitalists; in this respect the EU's use of the partnership agreement as a tool of pressure on Syria retarded the reform Europe ostensibly wanted.

Syrian Foreign Policy under Bashar

Syria's policy could have been transformed under Bashar and its position in world politics might have turned out quite different than it has. In the late 1990s, peace negotiations conducted under US auspices offered the prospect of a settlement with Israel. Bashar, bringing the outlook of a new generation, was in some ways predisposed to approach Syria's challenges differently. His political socialization took place in a radically different environment from that of his father and the regime "old guard." While the latter were socialized in the era of Arab nationalism, war with Israel, and non-alignment, their sons came of age in an era in which state-centric identities were fragmenting the Arabs, American hegemony and economic globalization had replaced the Cold War, and a peace agreement with Israel seemed attainable. While his father had remained hunkered down in Damascus and had little direct experience of the outside world, Bashar had acquired education in the liberal environment of the UK, married a British citizen of Syrian descent and, as president, travelled widely in Europe. Evidence of Bashar's modernizing worldview was his persuasion of his father to start opening Syria to the Internet on the grounds that a closed society was handicapped in the competitive world of globalization. It is worth cautioning, however, that Bashar's exposure to the West does not compare with that of most other Middle Eastern leaders. Moreover, the father-son relation, a presumably powerful socialization mechanism, would have committed him to the preservation of his father's Arab nationalist legacy while the apprenticeship he served under his father, including time within the military, would have socialized him into the code of operation of the establishment. And the legitimacy of the Bashar's presidency was contingent on faithfulness to the standard of national honour defended by his father, namely the full recovery of the Golan from Israel without being seen to abandon the demand for Palestinian national rights.

On the other hand, Bashar faced a deteriorating strategic situation. With its old Soviet patron gone and its newer American interlocutor turning hostile, Syria could no longer manoeuvre between rival global superpowers and lacked a great power protector. Bashar had immediately to deal with the consequences of the 2000 failure of the Syrian-Israeli peace process and inherited a Turkish-Israeli alliance that potentially put Damascus in a pincer. A burst of opposition to Syria's position in Lebanon followed Israel's withdrawal from the south in 2000. At the same time, the fragmentation of the Arab world made it harder to mobilize Pan-Arab political support or financing for Syria's policies.

Worse, Syria's military position was deteriorating. After the 1990s collapse of its Soviet arms supplier, it faced the degradation of its deterrent. The army's combat strength deteriorated dramatically during the 1990s, its Soviet equipment increasingly obsolescent, with Soviet/Russian demand for payment in hard currency and threatened US sanctions against Russian companies that sold Syria arms denying it enough ammunition and spare parts. These constraints on Syria's prospects of sustaining the conventional military balance with Israel, plus a growing technological and airpower gap with it, led its defence effort to take non-conventional directions. Hizbullah's capacity to fire rockets deep into Israel and to engage Israeli forces in asymmetric warfare became the first line of Syria's new deterrent. Syria's 1990 Gulf war aid windfall was invested in a second line deterrent of chemically weaponized missiles in hardened sites targeting all of Israel. Perversely, it was unilateral Syrian renunciation of this deterrent, crucial to maintaining the Syrian-Israeli peace, that the EU, at US urging, tried to make a condition of a Euro-Mediterranean partnership agreement with Syria.

Bashar's first response to this situation was to try to construct multiple alliances, at both the regional and the international levels, through which the pressures on Syria might be diluted and external resources accessed. He sought to improve relations within the region and particularly with Turkey and at the global level he sought a strategic opening to Europe and Syrian adhesion to the Euro-Mediterranean partnership, with all the more urgency as friction rose with the US. But the 2000 failure of the Syrian-Israeli peace process also triggered Syria's 2001 opening to Iraq under Saddam which would bring Syria, via a chain of events, into a conflict with the West that substantially diverted Bashar's foreign policy from his initial Westcentric path. Instead Syria ended up a partner with Iran in an axis of resistance locked in a struggle for the Middle East with the US and its regional allies. Bashar could not have anticipated this outcome when in 2000 US Secretary of State Madeline Albright attended the funeral of his father and welcomed his accession as a reforming president.

Between Militancy and Conciliation toward Israel

Bashar pursued an ambiguous policy toward Israel, reflective of his dual nationalist and modernizing impulses. Peace negotiations had broken off in early 2000 but on assuming power, he affirmed that Syria was willing to resume them if Israel acknowledged what Syria took to be the commitment made under Yitzhak Rabin to a full withdrawal to the June 4, 1967 borders on the Golan. But thereafter, the rise of Ariel Sharon to power in Israel pushed a settlement off the agenda and his repression of the Palestinian *intifada* inflamed Syrian public opinion against Israel. Bashar therefore revived Syrian militancy toward Israel, both to generate personal nationalist legitimacy essential to his power consolidation and to send the message to Israel that it could not enjoy a peaceful environment and still keep the occupied territories.

Syria returned to its earlier insistence that a Syrian-Israeli settlement had to be part of a comprehensive one that included a Palestinian state (briefly set aside after the Palestinians took responsibility, at Oslo, for their own destiny), called on the Arabs to support the Palestinian *intifada*, allowed Hamas and Islamic Jihad to maintain offices on Syrian territory even though these groups were involved in suicide bombings in Israel and supported Hizbullah operations against Israeli forces in the disputed southern Lebanon Shebaa Farms enclave. Israel, seeking to make this strategy too costly, twice bombed Syrian positions in Lebanon and in 2003 attacked what it said was a Palestinian training camp near Damascus after an Islamic Jihad suicide attack. As Syrian-Israeli relations deteriorated, anti-Syrian enmity grew in Washington, particularly evident in George W. Bush's support for these Israeli attacks on Syria. Syria facilitated the rocket armament of Hizbullah as a deterrent against the increased Israeli threat[12] and made massive arms deliveries to it during its summer 2006 conflict with Israel.

But Bashar still wanted a negotiated settlement with Israel and, also in part to disarm the US neo-cons after the US occupation of Iraq, he again offered to resume peace talks with Israel. The neo-cons, believing a peace settlement to be a benefit of which Syria was undeserving, discouraged Israel from responding, but Israel's failure to crush Hizbullah in its 2006 war (and to pacify the Gaza Strip), may have incentivized it to explore his offer and in 2008 Turkey began brokering informal discussions between the two sides; since an agreement would require keen US engagement, however, it would have to await departure of the Bush administration.

Defying the hegemon over Iraq

In 2000, when Hafiz al-Asad died, US-Syrian relations were still amicable; within a few years of Bashar's succession they had degenerated into an enmity that is not easy to explain given Bashar's Westcentric reform agenda. This was also at odds with the long recognition of the two sides that they needed each other: Syria saw the US, although Israel's main backer, as a necessary broker in a peace settlement and the US under Clinton had seen an Israeli-Syrian peace as pivotal to completing a "circle of peace" around Israel and empowering 'moderate' forces in the region. However, Syria was publicly blamed for refusing an Israeli offer regarding the Golan at Geneva in 2000, although in fact, as US participants such as Martin Indyk and Robert Malley later admitted, Israel retreated from its prior promise of full withdrawal to the 1967 lines. Nevertheless, the failure of the peace process interrupted the US-Syrian engagement that had paralleled it.[13] And with a settlement off the agenda, Syria ceased to be pivotal to US Middle East policy.

Most decisive in the decline of US-Syrian relations, however, was the rise to power in the Bush government of the Likud-linked "neo-cons" who had been advocating Israeli use of force against Syria, and once in power wanted to similarly use American power.[14] In Congress US politicians linked to the Israeli lobby began preparing economic sanctions against Syria, under the so-called Syria Accountability and Lebanese Sovereignty Restoration Act (SALSA), which the executive initially opposed but later accepted. For the neo-cons, Syria was a threat to Israel rather than a partner in the peace process and a Syrian-Israeli peace in which Israel would have to concede the Golan was a positive evil. As US-Syrian disagreements increased, so did the influence of the neo-cons overshadow that of US moderates who wanted to retain amicable relations with Syria. Thus, after 9/11 Bush announced that all states not with the US in the war on terror were foes, but Syria tried to take a middle ground supporting the US war on al-Qaida with valuable intelligence assistance, but objecting to the bombing of Afghanistan. Syria also objected to Washington's designation of what it regarded as national liberation movements--Palestinian militants and Hizbullah--as terrorists; it also regarded these groups as "cards" in the struggle with Israel and evaded US demands that it cease its support for them. The neo-cons made concerted efforts to paint Syria as a threat under the new doctrine that any state that both supported "terrorism" and had WMDs was a direct threat to the US and liable to suffer a US "preventive war." Neo-con John Bolton regularly raised the issue of Syria's chemically armed missiles, even though this was a purely defensive deterrent that enhanced the regional power balance and accused Syria of seeking nuclear weapons, although the CIA dismissed his claims. The US later supported a 2008 Israeli strike on what it claimed was a North Korean built nuclear facility. Its disinterest in Syria's proposal to turn the Middle East into a WMD free zone exposed its double standards: this would have put Israel's nuclear capability on the table while Washington's aim was to force a unilateral disarmament of Syria.

Iraq was, however, the main issue that led to worsening Syrian-US relations. Bashar's 2001 opening to Iraq coincided with the Bush administration's attempt to prevent Iraq from inching out of the isolation the US had tried to maintain since 1990. It objected to Syria's receipt of

Iraqi oil outside the UN oil-for-food regime even though US allies Turkey and Jordan received similar privileges. US Secretary of State Colin Powell mistakenly believed that he had obtained Bashar's agreement to put the proceeds from Iraqi oil in UN escrow accounts and when this did not happen Powell professed to find Bashar untrustworthy.[15]

The immediate catalyst of the crisis in US-Syrian relations was, however, the US determination to invade Iraq. At the UN and in the Arab League, Syrian diplomacy attempted to build a coalition to block or at least withhold legitimation from an invasion. Yet Syria, keen not to be isolated from "international legitimacy" voted for UNSC 1441, mandating the renewal of United Nations weapons inspections in Iraq, in the hope this might deprive Bush of an excuse for war; indeed US Secretary of State Colin Powell wrote a letter assuring Syria that the resolution aimed at a peaceful settlement of the Iraq WMD standoff. Bashar infuriated Washington when, in a famous interview on the eve of the war with *al-Safir* (on March 27, 2003), he observed: "No doubt the U.S. is a super-power capable of conquering a relatively small country, but...the U.S. and Britain are incapable of controlling all of Iraq."

Syria did little to actually oppose the US invasion. Security barons close to Bashar allegedly facilitated pre-invasion sales of arms to Iraq, which, although meant for Iraqi self-defence, were considered illegitimate in Washington. Riding the tide of anti-American fury that swept Syria and expecting that Iraq would hold out for months, the regime allowed the movement across the Iraqi border of thousands of Arab resistance fighters, many from northern Syria with its close ties to Iraq and concentration of Muslim militants. Once the Saddam regime fell, Syria also gave refuge to some Iraqi officials fleeing Iraq.

Bashar al-Asad's defiance of Washington over the war, in striking contrast to the appeasement of other Arab leaders, was no idiosyncratic choice but it did reflect Syria's Arab nationalist identity rather than a pure calculus of interest. There were many incentives for Syria to acquiesce in the invasion. Opposing it gave the neo-cons in the Bush administration the opportunity to depict Syria as a US foe. Hafiz al-Asad had been rewarded for siding with the US in the first US-Iraq war of 1990 with control of Lebanon, which Bashar lost for opposing the US in 2003. Had circumstances been similar Bashar probably also have bandwagoned with the US, but in 2003 they were entirely different: If in 1990 Hafiz had a US commitment to a vigorous pursuit of the peace process, in 2003 the neo-cons made sure no such offer was on the table. If in 1991, Iraq was the aggressor against another Arab state, in this instance an Arab state was the victim of aggression by an imperialist power. Indeed, Syrian public opinion was so inflamed against the invasion that regime legitimacy dictated opposition, a more important consideration for Bashar's unconsolidated rule than was the case for Hafiz in 1990.

But the risks were high. In the wake of its triumph over Saddam Hussein, Syria was in Washington's crosshairs as the last remaining voice of Arab nationalism. The neo-cons were keen for the US to make an object lesson of Syria to convey the message that Arab nationalism was very costly and clear the way for a pro-Israeli Pax Americana in the region. The US presented Syria with a list of non-negotiable demands that threatened its vital interests: to end support for Palestinian militants, dismantle Hizbullah, withdraw from Lebanon, and co-operate with the occupation of Iraq—in short, to give up its "cards" in the struggle over the Golan, its sphere of influence in the Levant, and its Arab nationalist stature in the Arab world. No Syrian government could accept such demands without a major *quid pro quo*.

The regime believed, in fact, that it could steer a middle way over Iraq between unrealistic defiance of US power and surrender to it. The US, Syrian strategists believed, could not as readily resort to military force against Syria as it did against Iraq: Syria was not subject to international sanctions, and the destruction of the regime would likely further spread the chaos and radicalism unleashed in Iraq. While the US could easily defeat the Syrian army, the real military costs would come from pacifying a conquered Syria where the US would be harder pressed than in Iraq to find collaborators and would have no comparable oil resources to fund its occupation.

Nevertheless, under US threat, Syria rapidly backed away from overt support for the resistance in Iraq. Syria also continually sought an accommodation with the US, using what it thought were bargaining "cards": depending on whether Washington respected its interests, it could either advance or obstruct US interests, given its status as a key to settlement of the Arab-Israeli conflict; its unique ability to restrain or unleash Hizbullah's proven ability to hurt Israel; the offer of intelligence co-operation against al-Qaida and its ability to contribute to the stabilization or de-stabilization of Iraq. But it was imperial overreach that ultimately gave Syria a certain space for manoeuvre between defiance and submission. The hegemon had expended a lot of soft power over Iraq and its military was so over-committed that it could not take on another war and occupation.

Still, under unrelenting pressure, Syria did make further incremental, but ultimately significant concessions to appease Washington: borders with Iraq were tightened, Hizbullah was encouraged to stop its campaign against Israeli forces in the Shebaa farms, and in 2005 Syrian forces were withdrawn from Lebanon. Believing that much of US animosity to Syria was propelled by the neo-con's Likud connection, Bashar tried to disarm them by proposing to restart the peace negotiations with Israel. However, since Bush's policy was not to offer inducements to "rogue states," these concessions only encouraged US hardliners to demand more. Washington succeeded in depriving Syria of some of the vital "cards" by which it exercised political leverage in regional politics and especially towards Israel, most notably its dominant role in Lebanon. Equally important the Bush administration's devaluation of the traditional goals of US Middle East policy, regional stability (for which the neo-cons substituted "creative destruction") and the peace process, correspondingly devalued the "cards" by which Syria could promise to deliver or obstruct these goals. The 2006 Baker Commission's recommendation that the US engage with Syria and Iran, an acknowledgement of imperial overreach, raised hopes in Damascus that were dashed by Bush's rejection of this advice.

Hanging on in Lebanon

Syria's role in Lebanon was another issue fraught with contention between it and the West, as well as pro-Western states such as Saudi Arabia. They viewed Syria's tenacity in defending its influence in Lebanon as obstructive and negative. As Damascus sees it, however, it has permanent interests in Lebanon. One relates to identity: Lebanon is seen as a detached part of Greater Syria, hence Syria's natural sphere of influence and also a country that must be brought to acknowledge its Arab identity and not become a Western outpost like Israel. Lebanon has also been a source of economic resources for regime patronage networks. Syria has vital security interests in Lebanon: it must not be allowed to become a base for forces threatening to the Syrian regime. This includes Syrian opposition elements that have sometimes made Lebanon a safe haven. It also includes keeping Israeli influence out of the country, and specifically the reconstruction of the Israeli-Maronite alliance of the eighties; the Israeli military threat to use Lebanon's Bekaa valley to attack Syria's Western flank must also be deterred, a main justification for Syria's troop presence there. Moreover, the Hizbullah-Syria alliance had become strategic for Damascus, with each supporting the other against common enemies. Hizbullah's ability to stand up to Israel is a pivotal part of the Israeli-Syrian power balance. Bashar developed close personal relations with and was said to admire Hizbullah leader Hassan Nasrallah and the enormous Arab nationalist prestige Hizbullah won in standing up to Israel also benefited its Syrian patron. Finally, Lebanon was one of Syria's strategic "cards" in any peace negotiations: Syria could both veto a separate Lebanese peace with Israel and help deliver Lebanon into an acceptable one; it could also keep a hand on the 'Palestinian card' through Lebanon or Hizbullah.

From the point of view of Damascus, the US and France set out to deprive it of its "cards" and sphere of influence in Lebanon. It was their attempt to undermine Syria's role in Lebanon, seen as a potential weak spot, that may have precipitated the assassination of former Lebanese prime minister Rafiq al-Hariri, which was then blamed on Syria and used to mobilize demands for its expulsion from the country. The idea that Lebanon after Syrian occupation would be neutral and independent was not seen as credible in Damascus: either it would be the sphere of influence of Syria or succumb to that of the US-French-Saudi axis or even be penetrated again by Israel—*their* Lebanese clients would dominate instead of Syria's. Lebanon also now came to be seen as the main instrument through which they could threaten the Syrian regime. The unprecedented use of international institutions against Syria has been very alarming for Damascus. UNSC Resolution 1559 calling on Syria to withdraw from the country and for Hizbullah to disarm was pushed by the US and France despite the reluctance of other Security Council members and despite the protest of the Lebanese government against this interference in its sovereign affairs and that it was a bilateral matter with no implications for international peace and security, normally needed to justify UN intervention. The unprecedented setting up of an international tribunal to investigate the Hariri assassination was seen in Syria as a tool of regime change. Lebanon was also seen as a battleground in a wider struggle for dominance in the Middle East between the US and the forces of nationalist resistance, led at the state level by Iran and Syria, with parallel struggles in Iraq and Palestine expected to be affected by the outcome in Lebanon. Although Syria understood there was no prospect, after its forced 2005 withdrawal, of wholly restoring its old role as arbiter of Lebanon, it was determined to blunt the advance of its enemies there.

Syria's strategy in this struggle for Lebanon included several prongs. The alliance with Iran was tightened. Keeping the Hizbullah card was seen as essential to making sure Lebanon would not become a platform for regime change in Syria. Hizbullah's ability to stand up to Israel in the 2006 war showed its special value in any peace negotiations and as a deterrent against Israel. The key to protecting Hizbullah was to restore the 'consociational' system in Lebanon wherein no key decisions could be made without a consensus of the major sects—thus institutionalizing a veto for Hizbullah. This was against the attempt of the Western-backed March 14th coalition to use their majority in parliament and government to push through policies inimical to Syria and Hizbullah.

This strategy carried considerable costs. Europe was alienated, over the Hariri affair in particular and, at US urging, suspended the Euro-Mediterranean partnership agreement Bashar had sought. "Moderate" Arab regimes, notably Saudi Arabia and Egypt were antagonized. However, the strategy seemed to pay off when Hizbullah's May 2008 power demonstration in taking over West Beirut broke the Lebanese deadlock and led to the Doha agreement on formation of a national unity government in which Hizbullah had a veto over policy and the election of a neutral (if not pro-Syrian, pro-Hizbullah) President, Michel Suleiman. Syria would not now likely be undermined from what Washington had considered its main point of vulnerability, Lebanon; however the Lebanese elections of June 2009, won by the anti-Syrian March 14 coalition, threatened to again disrupt governance by a national unity coalition and split Lebanon, in part over the role of Syria.

The domestic political consequences of the Iraq war

Bashar initially had hoped to expand political liberalization, at least to the extent that it could be made to support rather than undermine regime legitimacy, economic reform and his own power position. His authoritarian reformist faction was flanked by two other political tendencies which he had to master. Old guardists sought to preserve the role and privileges of the Ba'th party, the nationalist line and perhaps the populist contract with the people. The loyal opposition ultimately wanted a democratic transformation of the system, but sought to gradually advance it through a coalition with Bashar's modernizers. The Damascus spring of 2001, in which Bashar encouraged civil society to express constructive criticism, seemingly in an effort to foster forces that would strengthen his own reformist agenda against the old guard, suggested that a modernizer-loyal opposition coalition was possible. But when hard-line opposition elements framed the conflict in zero-sum terms (attacking the legacy of Hafiz) and put the spotlight on the corrupt activities of regime barons, the hard-liners in the regime were empowered and Bashar shut down the experiment. Western democracy, he asserted, could not just be imported and democratization had to build upon social and economic modernization, as in the Chinese model, rather than precede it – lest instability, a la Gorbachev, ensue. Indeed, if

Bashar's economic reform program entailed rolling back the social contract and entering a stage of crony capitalism, authoritarian rule would be needed to contain popular opposition.

At the same time, as the neo-cons trumpeted the US conquest of Iraq as a first step toward inspiring revolt against similar regimes across the region, Bashar laid down red-lines for the opposition: threats to national unity (by stimulating sectarian conflict) and any collaboration with foreign forces were unacceptable. Human rights campaigner Haitham al-Maleh and hard-line opposition figurehead Riyad al-Turk agreed that US pressures undermined reformers and enabled the regime to justify continued emergency powers.[16] The loyal opposition asked to be included in a national unity government to strengthen Syria against the external threat and there were good reasons for bringing it in: 'To stand up to the Americans you have to make internal changes and mobilize people around you,' said one analyst. 'If not, you have to follow the Americans...The regime...has not decided which way to go.' No opposition figure advocated submission to US demands to reduce support for Hizbullah or militant Palestinians. Syrians of all ages, sects and classes seemed to share a profound dislike of Bush for having attacked Iraq, as they believed, on behalf of Israel and to seize its oil. Some favourably compared their president's stands to the failure of the 'cowards who run the Arab countries' to stand up to Bush.[17] The Iraq war stimulated an Islamic revival and the regime tried to use it to strike a détente with Islamic forces that had long represented the main alternative to Ba'thist rule.[18]

The legitimacy of the regime must, however, have suffered from the foreign policy reverses inflicted by the US, given that this had long rested on its claim to act for Syrian Arab nationalism. If Hafiz was respected for his effectiveness on behalf of this cause, Bashar had to swallow several American and Israeli military provocations and Syria's forced evacuation of Lebanon. The mounting costs of defying the US stimulated growth of a 'little Syrian' identity. Yet the very fact that Washington targeted the regime for its stands on behalf of still popular *Arab* causes--its support of Palestine, its association with Hizbullah and its opposition to the invasion of Iraq--generated a certain solidarity between regime and people. Many Syrians, feeling victimized by the US-orchestrated global demonization of Syria over its Lebanon presence, rallied around the government rather than turning against it. Additionally, the chaos and sectarian conflict in Iraq, together with the fear--ignited by the Kurdish riots of 2003 and the rise of Islamic militancy--that the 'Iraqi disease' could spread to Syria, led the public to put a high premium on stability. This generated for the regime what might be called 'legitimacy because of a worse alternative.' However, the regime could not be brought to undertake political experiments that might constrain its monopoly of power at a time when it had to both cope with threat from without and push economic reform within.

From the "Struggle for the Middle East" to partial emergence from isolation

A major consequence of Syria's stands on the Iraq (2003) and Lebanon (2006) wars was a shift in regional alignments as Syria was estranged from its traditional Arab partners, Egypt and Saudi Arabia. Bashar was highly critical of their acquiescence in the US invasion of Iraq and they blamed Syria and Iran for the 2006 Lebanon war; the Saudis also blamed Syria for the assassination of their long time ally, Rafiq al-Hariri. Syria accused the Saudis of backing terrorist attacks in Syria "to ruin Syria's image as island of stability that the West should deal with." By 2006 Syria had became involved in a struggle for the Middle East between what some saw as two axes, a "moderate" one aligned with the US, backed by the EU and including Saudi Arabia, Egypt and Jordan and, on the other side, Iran and Syria, aligned with Hizbullah and Hamas, which stood for Arab nationalist and Islamic resistance to the US in the region and enjoyed wide support in Arab public opinion. Iraq, Lebanon and Palestine were the key battlegrounds between the rival alliances. As Syria faced isolation in the West as a "pariah" state, its links with Iran and the radical axis were strengthened.

Yet by the end of 2008, Syria seemed to have survived the Western campaign against it and relations seemed to improve. Even before that the manifest disaster brought on the US by the neo-cons' policies had led to the decline of their influence in Washington and a corresponding decline in US enmity toward Syria. Bashar outlasted his two main *nemesises*, Bush and Chirac, with both of their successors apparently abandoning their efforts to isolate the country. But the change of heart in the West toward Syria also resulted from a realization that the policy of isolating it was counterproductive. The 2008 shift in the power balance toward Syria in Lebanon precipitated a shift at the international level in which French President Sarkozy broke with the US policy of isolating Syria, the symbol of which was his invitation of Bashar to the Paris launch of his new European-Mediterranean union where Syria's accession to the European-Mediterranean partnership was again put on the agenda. On the other hand, relations with Egypt and Saudi Arabia were subsequently exacerbated by Syria's backing for Hamas in the 2008 war over Gaza and their ambivalent stance on the

Israeli invasion, although there were some signs thereafter that Riyadh and Damascus were trying to end their feud.

By 2009, Syria had managed to position itself between two networks: on the one hand, it was part of the Iran-led "resistance axis," a defiance of the West enabled by diversified economic connections to Asia and renewed security and economic relations with Russia (taking advantage of Georgian crisis); on the other hand, the Westcentric option had been revived: Western Europe, manifest in detente with France; in Turkish-sponsored peace talks with Israel; and in a cautious dialogue with the new Obama administration. If its interests were ignored or respected Syria could tilt one way or the other.

Yet, Syria still laboured under serious vulnerabilities. To advance economic reform and overcome the looming resource/ fiscal crisis, it accelerated its integration into the global economy through a kind of "Lebanonization" in which inward investment in tertiary and luxury businesses was prioritized. This, however, made the country more vulnerable to global economic pressure and turmoil in financial markets. Moreover, the departed Bush administration had engineered an institutionalization of Syria's "pariah-hood" that would be very hard to reverse. It has thus strewn several "mines" in the path of Syria's attempted integration into the global economy. US sanctions on the economy and particularly the Syrian commercial bank obstructed aspects of the regime's attempted global financial integration, discouraged companies from doing business in Syria and made more difficult and expensive the acquisition of key components needed for flagship sectors of the economy such as banking, oil, and telecommunications. The international Hariri tribunal constitutes a permanent threat that can be used to extract concessions from Syria by its enemies. The IAEA charges over an alleged nuclear site destroyed by the Israelis near Deir ez-Zor may likewise be used against Syria (while, typically, Israel's air attack on a sovereign country was ignored by the "international community.") Were these threats to the regime to be actively deployed, it would undoubtedly do whatever is needed to survive. In this respect, the "Qaddafi option"—surrendering its "cards"-- would only be possible in the unlikely event Israel was prepared to return the Golan. Its most likely response would therefore be to tilt away from the West and back to the resistance axis, again seeking to outlast its antagonists.

Syrian-US Relations under Obama

Before Bush, US-Syrian relations were amicable; will Bush's departure make much difference in repairing the serious rupture between the two countries? Syria gave the Obama administration a cautious welcome and Obama moved fairly quickly to explore the possibility of improving relations. Bashar told the Guardian (February 17, 2009): "We have the impression that this administration will be different, and we have seen the signals. But we have to wait for the reality and the results."

Indeed, the US seemed initially to continue the policy of Bush in setting conditions and making demands on Syria while expressing them in a less pre-emptory and more conciliatory way. In a 15 February 2009 meeting with Syrian Foreign Minister Walid al-Mouallem, US Assistant Secretary of State Jeffrey Feltman reportedly brought up the issues of Syria's support of terrorism, its efforts to obtain nuclear weapons, its involvement in Lebanon, and the deterioration of the human rights situation in Syria (*Al-Nahar*, February 27, 2009); he said afterwards that the U.S. had not yet reached understandings with Syria about all of these issues. John Kerry, chairman of the Senate Foreign Relations Committee, declared at a press conference in Beirut on his way to meet Bashar that Syria has to respect Lebanon's independence, advance a solution to the inter-Palestinian conflict and the conflicts between Hizbullah and the other Lebanese factions, promote the implementation of U.N. Resolution 1701 (on Syria-Lebanon relations), and change its behaviour towards Iraq (*Al-Hayat*, February 19, 2009.) In his meeting with Kerry, Bashar called on the U.S. to relinquish the "policy of dictates" that had proven to be ineffective, stating that dialogue was the only way to identify the real problems (*Al-Thawra*, February 22, 2009) After the meeting Kerry stated that despite the disagreements, there was a chance for genuine cooperation between the two countries on various issues (*Al-Watan*, February 22, 2009). The Lebanese daily *Al-Akhbar* (March 12, 2009) reported that the US offered to play a role in Israeli-Syrian negotiations, remove Syria from the list of states sponsoring terror, and lift the sanctions currently imposed on it if Syria severed its ties with Iran, Hizbullah, Hamas, and other Palestinian factions. The London daily *Al-Sharq Al-Awsat* reported that Syria had expressed a willingness to help in settling the conflict between Fatah and Hamas, in establishing a Palestinian unity government, and in arranging the release of Israeli soldier Gilad Shalit (*Al-Sharq Al-Awsat*, March 4, 2009). However, Asad's political and media advisor Buthaina Sha'ban said that improved relations with the U.S. would not be at the expense of Syria's relations with Iran, and added, "It is [also] time to stop telling

Syria and Iran to sever their relations with Hizbullah, Hamas, and the other resistance organizations." (*Al-Quds Al-Arabi*, March 19, 2009). Indeed, Syrian officials argued, "If the U.S. wishes ... to sponsor the peace process, it must be impeccably impartial and fair. To that end, it must declare that resistance is a legitimate right, and that terror and resistance are two different things." (*Tishreen*, February 21, 2009). Al-Mu'allem likewise called on the U.S. not to link its bilateral relations with Syria to the latter's positions on Middle East issues. *(Tishreen,* March 22, 2009).

Still, Syrian officials were conciliatory and optimistic. The Syrian Ambassador to Washington 'Imad Mustafa remarked: "There is much common ground between Syria and the U.S. as to ending the war in Iraq, attaining peace [in the Middle East], and restoring the legitimate rights of the Palestinian people. However, there are disagreements about the details and about the methods and mechanisms of implementation." (*Al-Thawra*, February 24, 2009). In an interview for *Al-Jazira*, Foreign Minister al-Mu'allem said that there were "some points of convergence" between the Syrian and U.S. positions regarding the security, stability, and unity of Iraq, and that Syria supported Obama's decision to withdraw from this country (*Teshreen*). He also expressed willingness to support the implementation of Resolution 1701 regarding Lebanon, and disclosed that, in accordance with it, Syria was forming a special team to demarcate the Syrian-Lebanon border (*Al-Akhbar*, March 12, 2009).

According to a senior Syrian analyst, the US and Syria agreed that terrorism and WMDs were a threat, and that Arab-Israeli peace was a shared interest. But they disagreed about the source of terrorism: for Syria, Israeli state terrorism was the threat while, as Syria saw it, the US deliberately obfuscated the distinction between terrorism and resistance to Israel by Hizbullah and Hamas. For Syria, the Israeli nuclear arsenal was the threat while the US was fixated on claims that Iran and Syria were trying to acquire WMDs. While Syria believed peace required pressure on Israel, the US wanted to get concessions from the Arab side.

For its part, Syria also had conditions for putting relations on a fully amicable footing. As a first step, it wanted the appointment of a U.S. ambassador in Damascus (*Al-Thawra*, February 25, 2009). It called for removal of Syria from the list of countries sponsoring terror, and the abolition of the Syria Accountability Act, which imposes US sanctions on Syria (*Al-Safir*, November 28, 2009). In addition, Syria appeared to believe its policy toward the US had paid off. As Syria's US ambassador argued: "Syria's winning card is [the fact that] it has not moved from its positions despite all the pressures it has been facing... The [fundamental] principles of [its] policy towards Washington have never changed, [even] in the most difficult circumstances" and Syria had never "submitted to this blackmail" (*Al-Watan*, February 24, 2009). Moreover, former Syrian information minister Mahdi Dahlallah put forward a sceptical view of the new administration: "The most important factor that brought about the change [in U.S. policy] is the Arab resistance camp, [comprising] Syria, the Lebanese and Palestinian resistance, and the Iraqi people, who refused [to accept] the occupation. Additional [factors] are the Iranian position, which refuses to accept the [American] hegemony, as well as the new Russian policy..." Had Bush been able [to implement] his policy without meeting opposition from anyone, the new administration would have continued the same policy... The change introduced by Obama ... does not stem from an [American] reassessment of its ideology ... but from [Bush's] failure to achieve the goals that the U.S. was – and still is – pursuing... *(Tishreen*, February 25, 2009). [This administration simply] realized that it cannot promote the totality of its interests in the region without a relationship with the Syrians..."

Nor were the Syrians sure that the Obama team would bring more than a change in tone. Syrian MP Khaled Al-'Aboud declared: "The U.S. insists on playing a role that, so far, has been too big for it. It has not yet grasped the facts or [acknowledged] the legitimate and unquestionable rights of the people of the region." For example, the U.S. continued to support the anti-Syrian March 14 forces in Lebanon as a tool to pressure Syria and sought to construct an Arab coalition to pressure Iran (*Tishreen*, March 10, 2009). One Syrian commentator wrote: "The ecstasy displayed by the Arab public as it followed Obama's victory is understandable: their hatred for Bush made them feel vengeful." The likelihood was, however, that Obama's more astute diplomacy and the better image he had secured for the US would merely reduce resistance to US power.

Indeed, Obama renewed sanctions on Syria for another year on the grounds that agreement had not been reached on dealing with "terrorism:" Syria was specifically accused of re-opening the routes for militants into Iraq. On the other hand, US Middle East envoy, George Mitchell visited Damascus as a prelude to starting up the Syrian-Israeli negotiations track. In his team was Frederic Hof, an expert on what a Syrian-Israel settlement might look like, with a reputation for scrupulous even-handedness toward the issue, a big improvement over the dominance of the US team under Clinton by friends of Israel such as Dennis Ross and Martin Indyk. In late June it was widely reported that the US would appoint an ambassador to Damascus although at the time of writing this had not happened.

The massive August 2009 bombings in Iraq which its Prime Minister Nouri al-Maliki blamed on Syria threatened to put Syria again at the eye of the storm. Prior to the bombings, Syrian and US officials had held discussions on an apparent common interest in the stabilization of Iraq, given the US decision to withdraw from the country. Syria's prime minister and foreign minister had recently visited Iraq and a Syrian ambassador was appointed in Baghdad. Maliki had himself just visited Damascus for talks on cooperation and although Syria refused his demand to hand over Iraqi Ba'thists residing in the country, the visit seemed to consolidate relations. However, after the bombings both countries withdrew their respective ambassadors amidst a public exchange of accusations. Given Syria's stake in good relations with both Iraq and the US, few objective Western analysts or Arab observers found the charge against Syria to be credible and most assumed al-Maliki needed a scapegoat for his regime's security failures. Remarkably, Iraq's presidency council disassociated itself from al-Maliki's charge. The US did not join in the accusations made against Syria, but the occasion was seized on by neo-con Eliot Abrams to attack the Obama administration for its policy of engagement, a reminder that Syria still has many enemies in Washington.

Conclusion

Bashar al-Asad's first term in office could hardly have been more turbulent. As his second term entered its second year, his foreign policy record looked far better than would have been anticipated a few years previously. According to the premier Syria watcher, Patrick Seale, he has prevented Lebanon from falling under the influence of a hostile power, resisted U.S.-Israeli hegemony by forging a counter-alliance with Iran and Hizbullah, and remained steadfast in backing the Palestinians. He had refused to compromise the Arab nationalist credentials on which the regime's legitimacy rested, had managed to insulate Syria from the chaos on its eastern and western borders and to evade US efforts to isolate and damage Syria's economy.[19] And the West, headed by a new American president, seemed to acknowledge that engagement with Syria could not be avoided.

---

[1] Hinnebusch and Quilliam (2006), 'Contrary Siblings: Syria, Jordan and the Iraq War,' In: *Cambridge Journal of International Affairs*.

[2] Patrick Seale (1988), *Asad: The Struggle for the Middle East*; Moshe Maoz (1988), *Asad, the Sphinx of Damascus: A Political Biography*.

[3] Yair Evron (1987), *War and Intervention in Lebanon: The Syrian-Israeli Deterrence Dialogue*.

[4] David Lesch (2005), *The New Lion of Damascus: Bashar al-Asad and Modern Syria*.

[5] Volker Perthes (2004), *Syria under Bashar al-Asad: Modernisation and the Limits of Change*.

[6] Ibid.

[7] David Lesch, op. cit.

[8] Samer Abboud (2009), *The Transition Paradigm and the Case of Syria*.

[9] Volker Perthes, op. cit.

[10] Ibid.

[11] Ibid.

[12] Flynt Leverett (2005), *Inheriting Syria: Bashar's Trial by Fire*, pp. 119-20.

[13] Ibid., 47-8.

[14] A 1996 document, "A Clean Break: A New Strategy for Securing the Realm," drafted by a team of advisers to Benjamin Netanyahu by subsequent Bush advisers Richard Perle and Douglas Feith called for "striking Syrian military targets in Lebanon, and should that prove insufficient, *striking at select targets in Syria proper*." Similar documents advocated the US use of force against Syria justified its possession of WMDs ("Is Syria Next?" *The Nation*, 3 November, 2003; Tom Barry, "On the Road to Damascus: the Neo-Cons Target Syria, *Counterpunch*, 8 March, 2004).

[15] Flynt Leverett, op. cit.

[16] *Financial Times*, 26 August 2003.

[17] Saul Landau, "A Report from Syria: Between Israel and Iraq...a Hard Place", www.counterpunch.com, 26 July 2003.

[18] www.csmonitor.com , 3 November 2003.

[19] "Rewards of Syrian Diplomacy", www.patrickseale.com/ 3 Jul 2009[0].

2
Syrian Foreign Policy Between Domestic Needs and the External Environment
Marwan J. Kabalan

Introduction

For the past eight years, Syrian president Bashar al-Asad has been trying to implement his vision of reform while minimizing political and social costs. Due to domestic and external constraints, the pace of reform has been slow. Syria's domestic politics, it must be recognised, has always been tied to its foreign policy, dancing more often to the tune of regional and international developments. On the other hand, many have argued that Syria's foreign policy is its main domestic export, that is, that its foreign policy has been exploited to access resources needed for domestic security. What is certain is that the inside and the outside are intimately related: Syria's domestic needs have in most cases shaped its foreign relations and regional alliances while the external context has intimately affected domestic policy.

Throughout the 1950s and 1960s, Syria relied heavily on the Soviet Union not only for security assurances but also for economic aid. As a result, Soviet-style planned economy was introduced and most of the big private businesses were nationalised. Improvement in the relationship with the conservative Arab regimes and the West in the 1970s led to the introduction of the first liberal measures in the country in two decades. This earned Syria also badly needed handouts to sustain its economy and support the ailing public sector.

During most of the 1980s, Syria's support of the Iranian revolution and in the war with Iraq deprived it of most Arab economic aid. Iran compensated for that in the form of cheap crude oil and other technical assistance.

The collapse of the Soviet Union and the bad shape of the Syrian economy played key roles in defining Syrian foreign as well as domestic policies in the post-Cold War era. Syria supported the US-led coalition to force Iraq out of Kuwait in 1991. This position allowed Syria to navigate safely in an unfavourable unipolar world and also to win generous economic handouts from Arab Gulf States. Syria also joined the Madrid peace process; hoping that peace with Israel would not only lead to regaining the Golan Height, but would also generate good economic opportunities for the country and increase foreign investment.

The honeymoon with the US and the relaxed regional environment led to the second wave of economic liberalisation in Syria. The Syrian-Egyptian-Saudi axis and the illusion that a peace deal with Israel was in hand led to further liberalisation of the Syrian economy.

When President Bashar al-Asad came to power in 2000, the regional and international settings seemed ripe enough to introduce far-reaching economic and political reforms. A year later the whole picture changed, however, leading to a shelving of most of the domestic reform programs. Foreign policy, Syria's main export since 1970, has not always been an asset. At times it became a liability and proved to be extremely risky especially when there was a conflict of interests with the dominant powers in the international system. Such was the case when Syria opposed the US invasion of Iraq and President Bush's Greater Middle East Plan.

As Syria established itself as the anti-US power in the region, the Bush administration contemplated regime change in Damascus. The troubled relationship with Washington and other key powers in the region made the Syrian regime feel quite insecure, with the result that it put most of the domestic reform measures on hold. One must not, however, put all the blame for the slow pace of reform in Syria on external factors and harsh regional conditions. There are indeed key domestic challenges that also played major role in hindering reforms; but, when survival, the bottom line and first priority for Arab states, is threatened, every other concern is relegated to the bottom of the agenda.

The impact of Regional and International Contexts on Reform under Bashar

For most of the 1990s and up until the US invasion of Iraq, Syria's relationships with the western powers, chiefly the US and France, could be described as cordial. President Jacque Chirac was the only western head of state to attend the funeral of the late Syrian president Hafez al-

Asad in 2000. He pledged to provide all sorts of support to help the new Syrian leader –Bashar – to steer a radical reform. The Clinton administration sent Secretary of State Madeline Albright to Damascus. In a symbolic gesture of approval of the succession process, she held a two-hour meeting with the new president. Syrian News Agency (SANA) described the meeting as "constructive and successful". Crown prince Abdullah of Saudi Arabia and President Mubarak of Egypt, Syria's two key regional allies, expressed also their support for the new leader.

Taking advantage of the hospitable regional and international environment, Bashar launched his reform project. He pledged to liberalize Syria's politics and the economy. The first six months of his tenure featured the release of political prisoners, the return of exiled dissidents, and open discussion of the country's problems. The changing regional and international contexts played key roles in slowing, at times, halting or even rolling-back Syria's reform process.

The September 11 attacks on the US brought fundamental change to US policy, particularly in the Middle East. Before 9/11, US strategy in the Middle East revolved around two key themes: maintaining the status quo; and relying on strong leaders to sell any peace deal with Israel. After 9/11, however, stability in the Middle East was no longer seen in Washington as an asset but a liability. In addition, as the peace process disappeared from the Bush administration foreign policy agenda, strong Arab leaders were not really needed to deliver peace. The "war on terror" became the driving force of the Bush administration and "constructive instability" was designed to act as its modus operandi in the Middle East.

How did this shift in US foreign policy affect its relationship with Syria and by extension Asad's reform plans? At the very beginning Syria made "let the storm pass" a principle guide of its foreign policy. Although it broke with this principle in opposing the invasion of Iraq, thereafter it hence tried to deflect the wrath of the Bush administration by providing minor concessions and expressing support for its "war on terror". Later on, Syria gave away more vital concessions but failed to elicit any reaction from Washington.

In the wake of 9/11, Syria anxiously watched Lebanon being moved from the sideline to occupy a centre-stage in Washington's policy to the Middle East. Hizbullah – on the US State Department list of terrorist organisations since 1984 – became a key target in the "war on terror". In the immediate aftermath of September 11 Syria tried - through a quid pro quo policy - to eliminate Hizbullah from Washington's target list. Damascus supplied Washington with "sensitive" information about Islamic activists; hoping that in return

Washington would ease the pressure on Syria and Hizbullah. It did not work out. The euphoria resulting from the quick collapse of the Taliban regime in Afghanistan lured the neo-cons in Washington to shift the focus to Iraq.

Irritated by Syria's opposition to the invasion of Iraq and by its continued support for Hamas and Hizbullah, the Bush administration gave the go-ahead signal for the Congress to pass the Syria Accountability Act. The Act, which imposed economic sanctions on Damascus, called for Syria to withdraw its forces from Lebanon, cease intervening in Lebanon's internal affairs and stop supporting Hizbullah. Lebanon became a key front in the arm-twisting between Syria and the US. Anti-Syria protests by Lebanese activists were, in the opinion of many observers, instigated by the US pressure on Syria. They were also seen as the beginning of a political struggle to decide on who will rule Lebanon in the coming years. Bashar spent most of his time at this stage trying to ward off mounting US pressure to "change the behaviour of his regime". Reform, as a consequence, was put on hold.

The Invasion of Iraq and Syria's Security Dilemma

The invasion of Iraq was the key bone of contention between Syria and the US. From the very beginning, Syria was hoping that the US would fail to control post-war Iraq and struggled to accommodate itself with the strategic change which made the US a key Middle Eastern power. In early April 2003, President Bashar al-Asad told the Lebanese newspaper *al-Safir* that he hoped the invasion of Iraq would fail and that "popular resistance" would prevent the United States from controlling the country. As for the choice Syria would make, then foreign minister Farouk al-Shara' told the Syrian parliament that his country has chosen to stand with "the Iraqi people and international legitimacy", which the US and Britain have discredited by invading Iraq without a UN mandate.

Syria's position was seen by many as an irrational defiance to US hegemony. Some tried to explain it on ideological grounds; that is to say: Syria, by reason of being the hotbed of Arab nationalism, has always been paranoid about "Western designs" to keep the Arabs weak and divided. This "paranoia" forced Syria to adopt anti-Western policies during the Cold War. But Syria's policy on the Iraqi crisis had nothing to do either with the legacy of the Cold War or the bitter experience of the colonial era. Syria's position was simply a response to domestic needs – both economic and political - and was envisaged in geopolitical terms, which were directly linked to its security dilemma. After all,

Syria supported the US-led war against Iraq in 1991 and dispatched 20,000 troops as part of the war efforts to expel the Iraqi army from Kuwait. Syria also participated in the Madrid Middle East peace conference and came close to cut a peace deal with the former Israeli Prime Minister, Yitzhak Rabin.

The ascendance of Benjamin Netanyahu to power in Israel put an end to Syria's endeavours to regain the occupied Golan Heights. Protracted economic crisis - as Arab financial aid dried up and oil prices plummeted in the international market - also contributed to Syria's own vulnerability. As a result, Syria was forced to look for other options to survive and -at the time - Iraq was the only one available.

Syria had no love for the former Iraqi regime. For more than three decades, relations between the two wings of the ruling Ba'ath party in Damascus and Baghdad were shaped by mistrust and animosity. In addition, the two regimes had been involved in numerous attempts and counter attempts to unseat one another. Syria also supported Iran in the eight-year war against Iraq, whereas Iraq backed the Lebanese anti-Syrian government of General Michel 'Auon in 1989-1990. One feature was, nevertheless, common between the two regimes, that is, the utmost pragmatism and flexibility. As a result, from 1997 Syria and Iraq came to see one another as possible allies. The late Syrian President Hafez al-Asad started cautiously, but steadily, developing relations with his lifelong enemy, Saddam Hussein. The ascendance of Asad's son, Bashar, to power hastened this process as the new president lacked the personal animosity which marked the relation between Saddam and his father.

Between 2000 and 2002 Syria tried to develop its political and economic ties with Iraq but was careful not to provoke the Bush administration. The 9/11 attacks provided Syria with a mixed opportunity to proceed in a quid pro quo policy with Washington. Damascus supported President Bush's "war on terror" and supplied the CIA with valuable information on Islamic activists; in return Washington turned a blind eye to the smuggling of Iraqi oil through Syria. Syria and the US were also at pain to hide their differences over the definition each gave to the activities of Hizbullah and Hamas.

The rapid fall of the Taliban regime and the shift in US policy from fighting terror to invading Iraq led to ending these tacit understandings.

Relations between the two countries reached their nadir over the UN Security Council resolution 1441 (urging Iraq to abstain from WMDs), which Syria, after long and painful arms-twisting, voted in favour of. Syria supported the resolution after being assured by French President,

Jacque Chirac, that it did not authorize an automatic use of force against Iraq without another UN resolution. Syria also played an important role in aborting US attempts to secure another UN resolution that authorised the use of force to topple the Iraqi regime. When the US decided to abandon the UN process altogether and go after Saddam, a clash of interests seemed inevitable. Syria could not but oppose the US-led invasion of Iraq and its policy was based on pragmatic grounds.

From a political and strategic perspective, Syria was almost certain that the war against Iraq was fought by the US on behalf of Israel. This was a perception that could not be easily dismissed given that the war was planned and advocated by Israel's friends in Washington. In a region that is still very much dominated by a realpolitik approach and a delicate balance of power, Syria feared that a US-backed military administration or a Karazi-like government in Baghdad would almost certainly place it in between two hostile powers: Israel and a pro-US Iraq. Syria was also concerned about the possible disintegration of Iraq and the likelihood of this affecting its own Kurdish minority. In addition, the war was seen in Damascus as an attempt to reshape the political map of the region in a way that suited Israel and the US. This fear mounted when former Secretary of State Colin Powell, in a testimony to the US Senate in February 2003, stated clearly that this was a key objective of the US war on Iraq. More important, perhaps, Syria feared that it could be next on the US hit list and Washington made no effort to calm these fears.

Economically, Syria had been benefiting from profitable relations with Iraq for several years. From October 2000 until the US invasion, Syria was receiving 200,000 barrel of Iraqi oil daily at low prices. This amount of oil allowed Syria to increase its share in the oil market and generate $2 billion annually of much-needed hard currency. The advent of an unfriendly regime in Iraq deprived Syria of this important economic privilege at a time it was most needed.

From a domestic perspective, the Syrian government could not ignore the anti-war sentiments of its own people. Bashar's regime was young and lacked the strength and experience of his father. A pro-US stand would have caused his legitimacy unbearable damage and could have placed him in a very weak position vis-à-vis the opposition. In Syria, Islamists, pan-Arab nationalists as well as remnants of the communist parties were all united in their opposition to the US war on Iraq. That war, as a result of the messianic tone of the Bush administration, was seen by most Syrians as a war against Islam. In addition, many Arabs, Syrians included, believed that the invasion of Iraq had nothing to do with an alleged Iraqi acquisition of weapons of mass destruction, but an imperial crusade to control Arab oil resources. Anti-American sentiments also run high when Syrians, like most Arabs and Muslims, held the US responsible for the killing of more than 3000 Palestinians during the al-Aqsa Intifada.

The US invasion of Iraq had a tremendous impact on Syria's domestic and foreign policies. Threat perceptions, resulting from US policy in the region, shaped Syria's regional agenda and affected its reform plans.

Lebanon and the US-French Understanding

During the first two years of Bashar's rule, Damascus had a friendly relationship with Paris. In 2002, Syria joined forces with France, Russia, Germany and China in the UN Security Council to prevent the US and Britain from passing a resolution to legalize the use of force against Iraq. A year later, however, Syrian-French relations started to deteriorate at an incredible pace. Friendship turned into animosity and suspicion replaced trust. So, what had instigated this shift?

It all started in November 2003 when president Chirac sent his political advisor, Maurice Gourdeau-Montagne, to Damascus to meet president Bashar al-Asad. At the time tension between Washington and Paris could not be cut with a knife thanks to Chirac's strong opposition to the Iraq war.Montagne told al-Asad that the Iraq war had changed the political map of the Middle East and that Syria thus possibly needed to reconsider its anti-war policy. Having realized that what has been done in Iraq could not be undone, the French wanted to mend relations with the US. Montagne told his Syrian hosts that that was also the position of Germany and Russia. Syria disagreed.

In June 2004 Chirac took advantage of his meeting with President Bush in Paris to commemorate the 60th anniversary of the Normandy landings to persuade him to move beyond their disagreements over Iraq and toward agreement over Syria and Lebanon. Chirac, through his close ties to former Lebanese prime minister, Rafiq al-Hariri, was the one who initially brought the US into Lebanon. Until Hariri's murder, the Bush administration had no independent Lebanon policy.In August 2004, Montagne paid a secret visit to Washington to follow up on the Normandy talks between Chirac and Bush. He and Condoleezza Rice, then national security advisor to President Bush, agreed to turn a new page in their relations and to co-ordinate their policies in the Middle East, especially in Lebanon. The two countries sponsored resolution 1559 in the UN Security Council, calling upon Syria to withdraw its forces from Lebanon. Syria sensed a shift in the policy of the great powers. The natural Syrian reaction was to consolidate its influence in Lebanon. Damascus felt that Lebanon should not be lost under any conditions. It hence, supported the extension to the tenure of its ally, president Email Lahoud.

The shift in French policy did not only affect Lebanon but other issues in the Middle East as well, causing further damage to its relations with Damascus. France and Israel set aside their animosity for the sake of a rapprochement. This was accompanied by a tilt toward US and Israeli priorities seeking the isolation and destabilization of the Syrian regime. France believed that its interests in the Middle East were no longer served by supporting the status quo in Syria. For France, the death of Yasser Arafat and the collapse of the Saddam regime marked the end of the era of Pan-Arabism. Chirac decided, hence, to embrace a different policy line in the Middle East, one that took into account the occupation of Iraq, the end of the Intifada, the collapse of the Arab state system, and the "lack" of reform in Syria.

The assassination of Rafiq al-Hariri gave Chirac a strong reason to break with the past, abandon Syria, ally himself with the US, and pursue a new Middle East policy. That policy led to the exit of Syrian troops from Lebanon.

Insecurity Prevails

The September 11 attacks on Washington and New York have been the single most important event in determining America's outlook toward the Middle East in general and Syria in particular. But even before 9/11, some in Washington had called for increasing sanctions and pressure on Syria, with some advocating forced regime change in Damascus and others conditional engagement. While each of these options had its proponents among US foreign policy elites, the most radical position was held by neo-conservative theorists who back in 1996 had recommended "weakening, containing, and even rolling back Syria" as a new national security policy to the Israeli Prime Minister Benjamin Netanyahu. Their vision for the Middle East envisioned creating a new political order based on tribal and religious lines in place of the strong secular regimes in Iraq and Syria. Under the Bush Administration, numerous neo-conservative foreign policy strategists came to hold positions of influence, particularly in the National Security Council, the Office of the Secretary of Defence, the Office of the Vice President, and within the President's advisory circles. To these hard-line Zionist advocates, both Jewish and non-Jewish, 9/11 provided a unique opportunity to fuse Israel's security preferences in the region with America's "war on terror".

President Bush's early call for the establishment of a Palestinian state after 9/11 was rapidly displaced by the interpretive logic of hard-line Zionism. With international attention focused on the U.S war in Afghanistan, Israel moved to devastate the civil infrastructure of the Palestinian Authority. The U.S administration did not object, thereby permitting Israel's colonial-zionist interpretation of terrorism to align itself with America's war on Al-Qaeda. This obfuscation established that America and Israel were pitted against the same terrorist threat and must both fight an existential war against irrational enemies; to negotiate with such enemies effectively amounted to rewarding terror. This view grew to be a dominant influence in the formulation of U.S Middle East policy. America set out on a course to uproot "rogue" regimes, either by military force, as in Afghanistan and Iraq, or through diplomatic isolation and political pressure, as in Iran and Syria. The U.S would not offer incentives to such states to induce positive changes; diplomatic engagement would be limited to pressure. According to its neo-conservative initiators, "constructive instability" was to alter the regional security environment to the advantage of both America and Israel.

During its first term, there was no solid evidence to support the claim that the Bush administration was seeking regime change in Damascus. Yet, the Iraqi file served to stigmatise Ba'athist Syria as a prospective target and to urge further sanctions against it. Essentially, the Bush administration could not resolve its internal differences over a coherent Syria policy, leaving it with an ineffective posture. In fact, the White House was able to agree only on a list of complaints about Syria's lack of cooperation, which it reiterated in largely unproductive diplomatic exchanges with Damascus.

Towards its second term, however, the Bush administration began to coordinate a joint policy offensive with France seeking to diminish Syrian influence in Lebanon and, ultimately, expel it altogether. To this end, Washington's "Syria Accountability Act" decreed economic and financial sanctions, while UN Security Council Resolution 1559 required Syrian troops to leave Lebanon and demanded the disarmament of all militias, a measure aimed at Hizbullah. Following the assassination of Lebanese Prime Minister Rafiq al-Hariri, the U.S withdrew its ambassador from Damascus and intensified its policy of isolation by encouraging the heads of state, foreign ministers, and presidents of other countries to boycott the Syrian regime. As part of the concerted Franco-American effort against Syria, the European Union suspended an initialled agreement with Syria over the "Mediterranean Free Trade Agreement". The policy of forcing Syria out of Lebanon had several aims: beyond targeting the Lebanese sources of Syrian income and foreclosing the prospective growth of Syria's economy, the U.S also sought to deprive Damascus of its Lebanese base for applying political and military pressure against Israel.

By that time, Syria had already been established as the key anti-US power in the region and was hence regarded by the Bush administration as a major obstacle towards pro-US change in the Middle East. The regime in Damascus was seen also as incurable and that something had to be done about it. The story of 1559 might have ended when Syria bowed to pressure and ordered the exit of Syrian troops from Lebanon, but next-steps were being cooked-up in Washington to finish off the other (Syrian) wing of the Ba'ath party. Those who wanted to continue the campaign in the name of freedom and democracy started to address the question of internal Syrian politics directly. President Bush and his policy advisors moved slowly, but steadily, towards adopting the following position: it is in US interests to attack Syria, not only for its foreign policy--for "occupying" Lebanon, or for troublemaking in the region--but because it treats its people in a repressive way and for resisting democratic change in the Middle East. US pressure on Syria mounted. Damascus was repeatedly accused of sending suicide bombers to kill US troops in Iraq, supporting "terrorist groups" in Lebanon and Palestine and spoiling US plans for a "New Middle East". As a consequence, Syria was enlisted in President Bush's "axis of evil", alongside Iran and North Korea.

The neo-conservative policy of non-engagement towards Syria did not succeed in modifying "problematic" behaviour by Damascus. On the contrary, since constructive channels with Washington were not available, Damascus cultivated a strategic relationship with Iran, as well as bolstered its support for a democratically elected Hamas and for Hizbullah. Furthermore, Iraq became a greater source of regional instability than before the US invasion, while Iran's influence in the region increased steadily. On the other hand, the Bush administration did succeed in facilitating the desired Syrian withdrawal from Lebanon and disrupted economic investment in Syria. Indeed, the Lebanon portfolio presented a policy theatre of special strategic importance to Syria.

For that exact reason, US-Syrian relations reached their lowest ebb in the July 2006 war when Israel, in co-ordination with Washington, sought to undercut both Syria and Iran's regional influence by trying—and failing—to break the backbone of Hizbullah. In September

2007, the Bush administration renewed its efforts to punish Damascus, hence, the Israeli air-strike inside Syria. The mystery about the target of the Israeli raid on Syrian territories caused a great deal of concern in Damascus. Syrian officials believed that the Israeli raid was nothing but the tip of the ice-berg of a grand US-Israeli plan to attack Damascus and dismantle the Syrian-Iranian alliance.

Shortly afterwards, the Bush administration activated a shelved plan to support the Syrian opposition abroad. Washington channelled millions of dollars to groups and individuals seeking to overthrow the regime of Bashar al-Asad. Alarm bells went off in Damascus when the National Salvation Front (NSF), a loose umbrella for Syrian oppositionists in exile, held its second congress in Berlin, electing its political bureau.

Syrian-Saudi Relations Turn Sour

Syrian-Saudi relations had been boiling beneath the surface since the assassination of former Lebanese prime minister Rafiq al-Hariri in February 2005. The Saudi government hinted at a Syrian role in the elimination of Hariri and joined forces with France and the US to expel the Syrians from Lebanon. The two countries also took different sides in the power struggle in the Palestinian territories. Syria supported Hamas whereas Saudi Arabia supported president Mahmoud Abbas of the Palestinian authority.

During the 2006 war in Lebanon, relations between the two countries reached an all-time low. While Saudi Arabia (along with Egypt and Jordan) criticized Hizbullah's July 12, 2006 raid into Israel as "reckless", Syrian President Bashar al-Asad cheered on the Islamist group, describing its resistance as "heroic". The differences over Hizbullah's raid broke into the open during the Arab league emergency meeting in Cairo in mid July. The foreign ministers of the two countries traded barbs over whether Hizbullah bore any responsibility for the escalation in violence that followed its capture of two Israeli soldiers. The Saudi foreign minister was quoted as saying that Hizbullah's actions were "unexpected, inappropriate and irresponsible". His Syrian counterpart, Walid al-Mouallem, lashed back, asking "How can we come here to discuss the burning situation in Lebanon while others are making statements criticizing the resistance". After the fighting ended, President Asad criticized Arab leaders, whom he refrained from mentioning by name, for failing to support the struggle against Israel. Riyadh took this attack personally and the Saudi-owned media retaliated with a barrage of anti-Syrian material.

The tension between the two countries seemed to have eased during the Arab summit in Riyadh in March 2007. King Abdullah received President Asad, who took part in the summit, and expressed his wishes to improve Saudi-Syrian relations. Syrians were also pleased by the King's opening remarks in which he criticized the US policy in Iraq and described the presence of its troops as "occupation". In the following months, an exchange of visits by senior officials from the two countries to translate the King's wishes into something real was expected. It did not happen.

The key reason that hindered rapprochement between the two countries was the growing alliance between Damascus and Tehran. Saudi Arabia was very disturbed by the Syrian-Iranian alignment and Iran's increasing influence in the region. It, hence, boycotted the March 2008 Damascus Arab summit. The absence of the Saudis annoyed the Syrian government, causing further tension.

Syrian officials believed that Riyadh may have taken the key step towards complete breakdown in the relationship between the two countries. Damascus thought that Saudi Arabia had decided to support the US efforts to isolate it and force it towards total submission. It also complained about Saudi support for anti-Syrian Lebanese politicians as well as playing host to Syrian oppositionists. Saudi Arabia, on the other hand, accused Syria of not being sensitive enough to its concerns on a number of regional issues, particularly its strong ties with Iran, lack of co-operation to solve the Lebanese crisis and its Iraq and Palestine policy.

In fact, Damascus and Riyadh have always been key players in what the late Middle East expert Malcolm Kerr called "the Arab Cold War", wherein the two countries have at several key points taken opposite sides (Kerr 1971). In the 1950s, Syria rallied around the pro-Soviet Egyptian regime, whereas Saudi Arabia sought protection from the Western camp. Relations between the two countries improved only after the 1973 Arab-Israeli war, to which Saudi Arabia contributed a small brigade on the Syrian front and imposed an oil embargo on western nations backing Israel.

Syria's honeymoon with Riyadh lasted until the Iranian revolution in 1979, which put the two countries once again in opposite camps. Syria supported the Khomeini government throughout the eight-year war with Iraq, whereas Saudi Arabia stood by Iraq and financed its military machine against the Iranians. The 1990 Iraqi invasion of Kuwait brought the two countries very close to one another. The Saudis watched with astonishment as Syria supported the US-led coalition to expel the Iraqis from Kuwait. The shift in Syrian policy led to the emergence of the tripartite axis, including Syria, Egypt and Saudi Arabia, which dominated Arab politics for the following decade.

The tripartite axis survived until the US invasion of Iraq in 2003. Despite of the fact that Saudi Arabia and Syria both opposed the US invasion, their policies diverged widely after the collapse of the Saddam Hussain regime. Riyadh accepted the US occupation as a fact; Syria rejected it and supported the Iraqi resistance. Their positions regarding Iran were however the key bone of contention between the two countries, reflecting both geopolitical and ideological disagreements. Geopolitically, Saudi Arabia was more concerned about Iran's regional ambitions and its quest for nuclear weapons. The fear that Iran might use Saudi Arabia's large Shiite community as a Trojan horse to destabilize the Saudi royal family was also a matter of great concern. Saudi Arabia also complained about Iran's endeavour to establish a Shiite-dominated government in Iraq and was seen largely as a key oil-exporting rival. By contrast, Iran is Syria's major and only ally in the region. Given its geopolitical location, Syria does not seem to be concerned about Iran's nuclear and regional ambitions. Syria fears Israel more than Iran and the alliance with it is seen by Damascus as fundamental to its national security and wellbeing. Syria neither seems to be bothered by the so-called Shiite crescent or Iranian revolutionary expansionism. However, the conflict with Saudi Arabia has inflated Syria's security dilemma, affecting both its foreign and domestic policies.

The Fall-out of the July 2006 War

The six-week conflagration between Israel and Hizbullah during July and August 2006 was characterized by the rivalling interests of numerous actors. Israel's desire to degrade Hizbullah converged with American and European interests in weakening Syrian and Iranian strategic power. For Syria, the hostilities served to remind the United States and Israel that neither country can solve its security problems in the region without a strategic understanding with Damascus. The largest military payoffs from the war were accrued by Hizbullah and its backers. While the militia's rocket arsenal unveiled an unprecedented first-strike capability, its field tactics and subterranean fortifications demonstrated that Hizbullah can damage and deter Israel. The handling of the hostilities by Israel's leadership exhibited a lack of sound contingency plans and severely tarnished its image of military invincibility. But while the Jewish state spectacularly failed to achieve its declared objectives, it did make important strategic and diplomatic gains regarding the pacification of its northern borders. Recognizing that a desirable military outcome would not be easily attainable without an arms embargo, Israel's campaign against Hizbullah pursued major non-declared objectives: creating a pretext for Lebanon's government to support an international mandate aimed at containing Hizbullah and facilitating a multinational force explicitly authorized to obstruct Hizbullah military activity; hence, UN Security Council Resolution 1701.

Israel's aims were not wholly achieved, however. As resolution 1701 lacks a UN-Charter Chapter VII mandate, peacekeeping forces are left subordinate to the authority of the Lebanese government. The security tasks of UNIFIL and the arms embargo imposed on Hizbullah would not be effective without the earnest cooperation of either the Lebanese or Syrian governments, each adversely affected by the hostilities. The war severely eroded public confidence in Beirut's ruling coalition by unmasking the supposed virtue of its US-backing as a mirage and showing Lebanon's interests to be sacrificed to Washington's regional goals. Hizbullah's performance, during and after the war, resulted in a major domestic victory and effectively blunted the March 14 coalition's enmity towards Syria.

Bashar al-Asad gained considerable political capital from the war. A host of diplomatic and military dignitaries, European, American and Israeli, have come out in favour of negotiations with Syria. To be sure, the prospect of 15,000 multinational troops operating south of the Litani River would hamper Syria's efforts to facilitate and coordinate pressure against Israel from Lebanese territory. Yet, amidst the new political fault lines in the region, Hizbullah's disarmament and the implementation of resolution 1701 would come about only as part of a broader political agreement in the region. This would require abandoning the discredited conceptual foundations of America's current Middle East policy and a more substantive vision for the region which included positive engagement with Syria.

Conclusion

Like many other countries in the region, Syria struggles with a range of problems that need to be addressed sooner rather than later. Some of these problems are of existential nature not only for the regime but also for Syria as a state and society. Many Syrian would rather blame the inhospitable international and regional environment for most of their country's key challenges, an argument that cannot be easily dismissed.

Its four-decade old rentier state system has made Syria almost completely dependent on foreign aid subject to political conditions. Throughout the 1970s, Syria survived on handouts from the oil-rich Arab states plus other forms of aid, including military support from the Soviet Union. After a short, but severe, economic crisis in the mid 1980s, the Syrian economy thrived again, achieving a growth rate of eight percent per year. This rate was attained partly because Syria itself became an oil exporter. Oil revenues enabled the government to inject great amount of cash into the crumbling public sector, pay for public services and delay economic and subsequently political reforms.

In the late 1990s, some economists started to raise the alarm at the speedily depleting Syrian oil reserve. By 2012, most experts believe, Syria will become a net oil importer. Given that oil income accounts for 20 percent of the GNP, 70 percent of exports and 50 percent of the central government revenues, the decrease in oil production will be extremely harmful for the Syrian economy. Moving from being self-sufficient to a net oil importer is a huge problem Syria faces today. Concerns over oil security are increasingly influencing Damascus's diplomatic and strategic calculations.

In addition, during his 30-year tenure, which lasted from 1970 to 2000, the late President Hafez al-Asad was widely acknowledged to pursue a skilful foreign policy that placed Syria at the centre of regional affairs, with a role that exceeded its military and economic weight. This role has at one stage become Syria's major commodity. It was often seen as key to stability or instability in the region. The dividends generated from adopting certain foreign policies had however made Syria less inclined to pursue far-reaching reforms at home.

After the September 11 attacks on the US, the Bush administration pursued a policy resistant to a quid pro quo style in dealing with Syria. It has also discouraged foreign investment in Syria by adopting the Syria Accountability Act. In order to win Syria as a strategic ally, Iran tried to play the role of a patron. Yet, given Iran's problematic relations with the rest of the world and its own economic difficulties, it could not provide what Syria really needed.

Threat perceptions, mounting pressure and isolation by the US, and cold relations with most of the Arab world, had affected Syria's reform project, creating a less friendly environment to liberalise the economy and the political life. Yet, crises do sometimes produce positive side effects. Isolation, external pressure and the lack of foreign aid should act as a catalyst rather than a hindrance to reform. Damascus is no longer in a position to bury or ignore problems.

And yet, if one insists that domestic reforms cannot be undertaken unless more favourable external conditions are in place, that assumption too is outdated, in view of the improvement in Syria's regional and external environment. After seven years of reacting to foreign threats, Syria has weathered most of the fall-out resulting from the September 11 attacks on the US. It remains to be seen, however, how far Syria can go in pursuing its domestic reforms under the new conditions.

3

The Role of Bashar al-Asad in Syrian Foreign Policy
David Lesch

What does Bashar want? An anecdote from one of my meetings with
Bashar al-Asad provides some insight into this. A Bush expletive aimed
at Syria in a discussion with PM Blair during the G-8 summit meeting in
the context of the Israeli-Hizbullah war of summer 2006 had been
caught on tape. Bashar's response essentially was that Syria wants to be
taken seriously, wants to be respected, wants a seat at the diplomatic
table, and will do what it can within a certain range of options to get
there in ways that Syrian policy makers *think* are calibrated. As Bashar
emphatically said in his interview with *The Guardian* appearing on 17
February 2009: "We are a player in the region. If you want to talk about
peace, you can't advance without Syria."

It is thus a pity that the US image of Bashar was so skewed and
unrealistic at the beginning of his tenure in power, a factor in the
dramatic souring of US-Syrian relations. Certainly he was
underestimated, seen as politically inexperienced, a computer nerd and
ophthalmologist who liked Phil Collins music. There was no way he
could meet the high expectations in the West given the dilapidated,
broken-down country he inherited and the regional and international
baptism by fire he immediately encountered. Much of the congressional
testimony regarding Bashar surrounding the Syrian Accountability Act
in 2002-2003 was grossly ill-informed. Congress was in the post 9/11
"more anti-terrorist than thou" mode so they hopped on the anti-Syria
bandwagon, which was an easy thing to do at the time. Bashar has been
fighting that negative image ever since. The Syrians are typically bad at
public diplomacy in the West, although Bashar is better than his father.
Unfortunately, Bashar did not adequately adjust to the shifts in US
foreign policy under Bush. At times, he did not help matters with his
sometimes less-than-prudent comments made for domestic and regional

consumption which fed into the construction and confirmation of the negative image of Bashar and policy against Syria that was going on in Washington at the same time. This period led to a perceptual gap that still exists and must be overcome, a kind of anti-Syrian perceptual inertia that exists in Washington. A similar deep-seated distrust of Washington has congealed in Damascus.

Although Bashar has a progressive and modernizing orientation on some, notably domestic issues, we must remember that he is Hafiz al-Asad's son in more ways than one. He spent a mere 18 months in London studying ophthalmology. He is a child of the Arab-Israeli conflict; he is innately designed to protect traditional Syrian foreign policy interests.

I have personally seen him grow into his position over the years from being a bit unsure of himself and the world to being rather cocky at times; indeed, I saw him during the 2007 election/referendum, and he was almost cathartically exuberant over the outpouring of support for him, no matter how much it was orchestrated rather than genuine. That was the first time I got the feeling that he was making that shift from a possibly transitional authoritarian figure toward a lifetime appointment in power. Of course, this transition is no surprise as he has been on the upswing since the low point of the Mehlis report in late 2005. This is due in part to his own maneuvering, not to be underestimated, and his riding the concurrent upswings over the last few years of Iran, Hizbullah, and Hamas as well as benefiting from US problems in the region. In a way, he chose the winning side, or at least the more popular side, and he feels somewhat vindicated. He has successfully broken out of the US imposed isolation, with the US itself seemingly left to decide how much it wants to seriously engage with Damascus.

Let there be no doubt that Bashar is securely in power (and I was saying this during the heyday of the Mehlis report in late 2005, when the US and the exiled Syrian opposition seriously overplayed their hands). He built up an aquifer of support in Syria and in the region from keeping the country together despite external pressures and instability in neighboring countries, and from being perceived as not having caved into the American project in the region, particularly in Lebanon. He effectively funneled the expected nationalist response to this pressure and the need for resistance into support for the regime that has empowered the regime to quell domestic dissent and promoted Bonapartist tendencies in the presidency.

Bashar does not, however, have absolute authority. It would be wrong to see the Syrian regime, or the Syrian security apparatus, as a tightly knit, well-oiled, hierarchical machine. On a number of domestic issues of varying levels of importance, the right hand of the government does not know what the left hand of the *mukhabarat* is doing, and vice versa. Even though it is a neo-patrimonial regime (i.e. a system of rule based on administrative and military personnel who are responsible only to the ruler and on the allocation of resources establishing pervasive clientelist networks), Bashar has to reach consensus, negotiate, bargain, and manipulate the system. Implementation of domestic policy issues is a serious problem in Syria. Bashar is fighting against systemic, institutional, bureaucratic and cultural inertia. Also he inherited an array of Faustian bargains made under his father, i.e. unswerving loyalty to the leader in return for his casting a blind eye toward personal enrichment and corruption, that sometimes has the regime sincerely saying and wanting to do one thing, while actions by important groups connected to the regime, or actually in the regime, do something quite different. There is nothing that Bashar can do at times without undercutting his support base, something especially risky in a threatening regional environment.

Bashar has, however, acquired control over foreign policy decisions, which was not always the case, with the major turning point being the 2005 withdrawal from Lebanon and the exiling of Khaddam; in a sense, he lost Beirut and the network of interests stretching from there to Damascus, but in cutting these links gained full control in Damascus. The decision-making process remains a rather ad-hoc response to challenges and threats, without long term strategic thinking and reliant therefore on traditional modus operandi. There is no national security council-like mechanism coordinating policy; instead, there seem to be informal committees that focus on various foreign policy issues. Despite this ad-hocism, Syrian officials have a way of getting in line with regime policy, mimicking declarations and pronouncements often word by word. On some issues, it seems that Bashar tries to balance Walid al-Mouallem and Farouk al-Shara', as with the IAEA investigation in which Walid won on allowing them into the country while Farouk won in not allowing any media coverage while they were there. While many in the West see Syria's ties with Hizbullah, Hamas, and Iran as a liability and obstacle to rehabilitating Syria's international position, Bashar actually sees them as potential assets. In this respect Bashar insisted to me that Syria's support for Hizbullah and Hamas have nothing to do with Iran, with whom Syria has ideological differences, and are rather cards in the peace negotiations with Israel. With Syria it is all about leverage and bargaining chips, and it is a relatively weak country with few arrows in its quiver, so it is not about to give them up, certainly not before any peace negotiations begin. On the other hand, if

Syria is given a real seat at the table, which finally seems to be happening under the stewardship of the Obama administration, Bashar sees his country as a conduit in a positive-influence process, a facilitator in resolving regional conflicts or moderating regional instabilities.

This is certainly how Bashar has tried to position Syria, or at least how he wants it to be perceived, that is, as a facilitating element, and a problem solver, not a problem seeker. Syria sees its ability to create problems, which it had every incentive to do when threatened, as translating into providing it with the ability to solve problems when its interests are respected. And Syria is uniquely placed to play this role, as it is the only major Arab country to be able to play both sides of the fence. On the one side, it has been the cradle of Arab nationalism and at the forefront of opposition to Israel and to the US invasion of Iraq which gives it credibility with radical forces in the region. Indeed, if Syria is to keep the role of a facilitator, this requires it to have good ties with both pro- and anti-Western forces; otherwise, it becomes less useful in the regional and international arena. So, one should not expect Syria to cut ties with any of the resistance groups in the near future. Indeed, insofar as Syria moves closer to the West, it risks losing its influence with these forces and with Iran, requiring a delicate balancing act.

Yet on the other hand, Syria has often tilted toward the West or the moderate forces and it can make a credible claim to be able to serve presumed Western interests in regional stability if its interests are respected. In 1991, it sent troops to fight alongside US troops in the Gulf war and thereafter engaged seriously in direct talks with Israel during the US-sponsored Madrid peace process in the 1990s. There was intelligence cooperation with the US on Islamic jihadist groups, in 2001-2003 after 9/11, when Islamic extremism was seen as the biggest threat to both countries; only when the US became the greater threat to Damascus did this end and Syria moved closer to Iran. Syria can enhance Iraqi stability and security. There could be low-level cooperation over Iraqi refugees in Syria: Bashar told me he would like US help in funding the building of schools for Iraqi refugee children to keep them from going in a counterproductive direction. Turkish mediated exploration of the terms of peace negotiations with Israel were started, possibly within the framework of an international peace conference a la Madrid in 1991, this time based at least in part on the 2002 Saudi-Arab League peace initiative. Syria could contribute to a regional security plan à la the Damascus Declaration after the first Gulf war, which would first require improvement in what has been an antagonistic relationship between Saudi Arabia and Syria over the last few years.

Despite what Syria sees as attacks against it--from the Mughniyeh assassination in February 2008, to the Israeli strike against the suspected nuclear site in September 2007, and to the US cross-border raid in October 2008--Bashar has not allowed such incidents to spiral out of control or rupture any chance for improving his relationship with Europe and the US, especially as it became clear that Obama would win the election and offer new opportunities for a dialogue. This reflects in one sense how weak Syria is at the level of direct military confrontation. But it also reflects a far-sighted strategic vision, a product of what Bashar has learned over the years which, for the time being, is shaping Syrian foreign policy.

On the other hand, he certainly feels somewhat empowered politically and in no hurry to move quickly, although Syria's poor economic situation may dictate that Bashar cannot wait too long. He waited for Chirac to leave and it worked out; he waited for Bush to leave, and it worked out; hence he feels he can take a wait and see approach to assess the Obama administration's priorities. He will also wait to see how the Israeli political situation plays itself out. He is not going to rush into anything with what he perceives to be a weak Israeli government; as he told me on one occasion, a strong Israeli government (of any type) can make peace or war; but a weak Israeli government can only make war. In October 2008 he told me that he did not want to elevate the indirect discussions with Israel to direct negotiations without assurance of success; he said that he was "new" to this game, that it was his "first time" at this, so he could not afford to fail.

What complicates these negotiations, as always, is the parallel Palestinian-Israel "track." While Bashar would be very reluctant to sign a Syrian-Israeli accord ahead of a Palestinian-Israeli one, he did often mention to me that they do not have to be lock-step with each other. A Palestinian Authority official recently stated that the Syrian-Israeli track need not be harmful to progress on the Palestinian-Israeli track, and rather that the former could actually help the latter.

For Bashar, the Golan is the be all and end all result of being at the diplomatic table. He said to me in summer 2006 with great emotion that "I would be a hero" if he achieved the complete return of the Golan, intimating that this would provide him with the necessary legitimacy to advance regional peace and stability as well as domestic reform. In this sense, the systematic ingraining of the return of the Golan in the minds of two generations of Syrians, while being something of an obstacle to peace in the past, can actually work in favor of an agreement today. The Syrian regime believes it would empower it to assume responsibilities regionally and deliver reforms domestically as a result of peace.

Potential obstacles to Syria assuming such a positive role are the web of UN resolutions, the UN Hariri tribunal, IAEA investigations, the US sanctions, and the State Department list of countries that sponsor terrorism. Although much of this was initiated under Bush as instruments of pressure on Syria, they have a life of their own now, especially the UN tribunal which could obstruct long-term normalization of Syria's international position. They also mean that the Obama administration cannot move rapidly toward improved relations with Syria or into mediating a Syrian-Israeli peace. They coincide with powerful anti-Syrian elements in Washington in and outside of Congress, something of an anti-Syrian inertia, and a legacy of mistrust on both sides from the Bush years. But if there is the will in Washington, these issues could be separated from political engagement: even Saad Hariri mentioned that political engagement with Damascus could proceed along with the Tribunal—at least for a time.

It must be noted, however, that Syrian officials had a very negative view of Bill Clinton's Middle East negotiating team, a reality which has been overshadowed by their even more negative view of the Bush administration; if much of the Obama negotiating team is simply a reconstitution of the Clinton team, the Syrians will remember their past experience and go slowly until they see tangible US commitment.

The Obama administration seems to have recognized the importance of improved relations with Syria. It announced in June 2009 the return of the US ambassador to Damascus, a post left vacant since the Hariri assassination in 2005. The US apparently learned from the French example of measured quid pro quos with Syria, especially related to Lebanon. The re-establishment of a US-Syrian dialogue has provided a more favorable diplomatic environment for cooperation at many levels, including re-starting Israeli-Syrian negotiations, although the right-wing composition of the current Israeli government may work against this. In spite of this improved climate, the Syrians continue to get different signals from different parts of the administration, a fact of life that confused them a great deal during the George W. Bush years.

The US and Syria need to re-establish trust through dialogue, measure each other's intentions, and take small steps that could lead to bigger ones. Without investing much political capital the Obama administration could improve relations by simply letting nature take its course by refraining from obstructing in the way Bush did Syria's reintegration into the regional and international communities. But if it has the ambition to seriously give some new momentum to the stalled Arab-Israeli peace process, one necessary strategic move would be to develop a cautious partnership with Syria.

4

Inching Out of Isolation: Managing a Different Relationship with Syria[1]

Bassma Kodmani

For Syria, half a decade of difficulties appears to be over. On the economic front, the financial situation has hardly been affected by regional difficulties. This does not mean that the economy has improved but the flow of money has allowed the president to show some "largesse" by increasing wages of government employees and reducing taxes on corporations. The current financial crisis is only starting to hit. Its first impact is visible on the reduction in remittances transferred by Syrian workers in the Gulf countries.

On the political front, the opposition has almost entirely lost the narrow space that had existed in previous years. The departure of Syrian troops from Lebanon coincided (and this is not entirely a coincidence) with the silencing of opponents in a moment of vulnerability for the regime, when it was under strong attacks from Arab and Western countries. Unlike in many other Arab countries, political prisoners in Syria are not of the radical type, defiant of political order. They are moderate, reasonable democrats who were calling for peaceful change. The profiles of the political prisoners reflect the fierce nature of the regime, and its lack of tolerance of any form of protest, even when activists seek to engage in a dialogue with the government. The opposition is ostracized and choked. It is in disarray and divided on strategies for survival. But the major disagreements among opposition groups emerge around Arab issues rather than domestic issues: on attitudes towards Hamas and in face of the Gaza disaster. While some thought the opposition should continue its struggle for domestic reforms, others called for halting expressions of protest in order to show a unified "patriotic" position of support for the Palestinians under attack in Gaza.

The pattern of opposition in future is shaping up: there will be little underground activity as there is no support for it within the population which is most concerned about stability. The Muslim Brothers lost too much in the eighties and now see underground opposition as a failed strategy. Given that there is no space for opposition inside, the opposition is organizing outside the country, mainly in Lebanon and in Europe (for example, a new TV station was announced by the coalition of the Damascus Declaration). In brief, the opposition has little support inside, at least for now. It might become more significant if the domestic situation worsens, and if outside support becomes acceptable to public opinion. But the Syrian public has an acute sense of vulnerability and the belief that the country is the object of conspiracies is widespread. Even if large sections of the population have no respect for the rulers, they cannot contemplate the idea that outside players might have a positive role: "Our rulers may be thugs but they are our thugs" is the common thinking. However, the government in Damascus was confronted with the Sunni Jihad challenge, which is partly a fall-out of the war in Iraq, and partly of Sunni-Shia tensions in Lebanon.

Syria's Foreign Strategy in 2009

Syria has always worked through its regional environment. It is probably the Arab state most embedded in its regional environment, a strategy that has enabled Syria to sustain isolation and, when time comes, to cash in on the assets accumulated. During the Cold War, Syria learnt not to make itself dependant on outside powers.

Lebanon: The recovery of Syria after the big blunder of Lebanon and the withdrawal of Syrian troops is remarkable. 2008 was a year of regaining some ground in the country: Hizbullah's coup de force in Beirut in spring was followed by the Doha compromise agreement that gave Syria's allies a clear advantage by securing veto power for them within the Lebanese government. Doha was widely perceived in Damascus as a success for Syria in that it brought satisfaction to its Lebanese allies. Doha was a renewed recognition by the Arab countries that Syria has legitimate interests in Lebanon. After the election of Michel Suleiman, one of the first statements of the new president was about Lebanon's strategic doctrine and the need to coordinate with Syria in the process of redefining it. Thus, the new president was acknowledging that Lebanon is part of Syria's strategic space.

Syria chose not to intervene in any visible manner during the elections in Lebanon in June 2009 and emphasized instead that this was a strictly internal matter. But the difficulties that the designated Prime Minister Saad Hariri is encountering in forming a new government and the numerous visits to Damascus by Lebanese politicians are a sign of Syria's renewed (or uninterrupted) meddling in Lebanese affairs. It is as if Damascus chose to allow the election process to take place smoothly while remaining confident that it can later neutralize any gains that its Lebanese foes and their allies think they have achieved.

Palestine: Hamas and Hizbullah have given new strategic depth to the Palestinian question, a strategic depth that is no longer Arab but Islamic. While some might think that this is potentially uncomfortable for the rule of the minority in Syria, in fact it allowed Syria to recover its traditional position as the stronghold of steadfastness. The fact that this new resistance is both Sunni and Shia makes it even more comfortable as Syria can present itself as championing a sacred alliance for the just cause of Palestine. In this context, it is not easy to imagine that Syria will give up support to Hamas and Hizbullah. The cost in terms of Syria's strategic posture would be too high. Syria cultivates its image as the only Arab country that has not capitulated and abandoned the Palestinians for peace with Israel. Its priority for some time to come remains to accumulate assets and Hizbullah and Hamas are its key strategic assets.

Iran: In the early period of Bashar, his lack of experience (and the Bush administration's attitude towards Syria) led him to put Syria under the umbrella of Iran and, with this protection, he developed his understanding of regional and international politics. He made mistakes, paid the price, and learnt lessons: he learnt for instance why the moderate Arab camp matters and why he needs to balance his relations with Iran with links to them. Damascus was ready to make this move before the advent of the new administration in the United States. Iran was a looser of Gaza because the military option (Hamas's rockets on Israel) proved to be a non-strategy. Hamas is now seeking national unity. It sees the opportunity of coming back into a political process from which it has been excluded since the summer coup of 2007. While Syria favors a national unity government in Palestine, Iran is already expressing some unease and saying that "the Palestinian issue is not only Arab," i.e. it is also Islamic.

Israel: Will Netanyahu offer something interesting to Syria? Will the United States be tempted to support a separate Israeli-Syrian track and neglect the Palestinian issue? Due to Syria's strategy of embeddedness, the Golan issue will be difficult to separate from the Palestinian issue. Therefore, a peace strategy vis-à-vis Syria is more likely to be effective if it takes a regional approach. Alternatively, Syria might well decide to pursue negotiations with Israel in view of defining the full terms of a settlement on the Golan but would probably "shelve" the agreement and avoid the obligations that will result from signing it, until serious progress is made on the Palestinian issue.

Conclusion

Syria has managed to contain the multitude of threats issuing from its environment and Bashar has learned to fine tune his balancing acts in the region. On the other hand, there has been no major positive transformation in Syria's position, hence no major change in its strategy. It is unlikely to abandon its alliances with Hizbullah, Hamas or Iran without a settlement with Israel, while a Syrian settlement with Israel probably depends, in turn, on parallel progress on other tracks, notably in Palestine, but probably also in Lebanon and in US-Iran relations. The conflicts of the region are a seamless web, the strands of which it is almost impossible to unpick and separate.

---

[1] This is based on a presentation delivered at the annual Paris joint meeting of the Centre for Naval Analysis and the Forum du Futur 05/03/09.

Bibliography

Abboud, Samer (2009), "The Transition Paradigm and the Case of Syria," in *Syria's Economy and the Transition Paradigm,* St Andrews Papers on Contemporary Syria, St. Andrews.

Barry, Tom "On the Road to Damascus: the Neo-Cons Target Syria", *Counterpunch,* 8 March 2004.

Evron, Yair (1987) *War and Intervention in Lebanon: The Syrian-Israeli Deterrence Dialogue,* Baltimore: Johns Hopkins University.

Hinnebusch, Raymond and Neil Quilliam (2006), 'Contrary Siblings: Syria, Jordan and the Iraq War,' In: *Cambridge Journal of International Affairs,* 19:3, 2006, pp. 513-28.

Kerr, Malcolm (1971): *The Arab Cold War. Gamal 'Abd al-Nasir and his Rivals, 1958-1970.* London: Oxford University Press.

Landau, Saul (2003) "A Report from Syria: Between Israel and Iraq...a Hard Place", *Counterpunch,* 26 July 2003.

Lesch, David (2005), *The New Lion of Damascus: Bashar al-Asad and Modern Syria,* New Haven: Yale University Press.

Leverett, Flynt, (2005) *Inheriting Syria: Bashar's Trial by Fire,* Washington, DC: Brookings Institute Press.

Maoz, Moshe (1988), *Asad, the Sphinx of Damascus: A Political Biography,* New York: Grove Weidenfeld.

Perthes, Volker, (2004) *Syria under Bashar al-Asad: Modernisation and the Limits of Change,* Adelphi Papers London: Oxford University Press for IISS.

Seale, Patrick (1988), *Asad: The Struggle for the Middle East.* Berkeley, CA: University of California Press.

Newspapers

Al-Akhbar (Beirut, Lebanon)
The Financial Times (UK)
The Guardian (UK)
Al-Hayat (Riyadh, Saudi-Arabia)
Al-Nahar (Beirut, Lebanon)
Al-Quds Al-Arabi (Palestinian-owned, London, UK)
Al-Safir (Beirut, Lebanon)
Al-Sharq Al-Awsat (London, UK)
Al-Thawra (Damascus, Syria)
Tishreen (Damascus, Syria)
Al-Watan (Damascus, Syria)

About the Authors

Raymond Hinnebusch is professor of international relations and Middle East politics and director of the Centre for Syrian Studies at St Andrews University, Scotland. He is the author of numerous articles and books on Syria including *Syria: revolution from above* (Routledge 2001) and "Modern Syrian Politics" (in: *History Compass*, 6/1, 2008).

Marwan J. Kabalan is Lecturer at the Faculty of Political Sciences, Damascus University, an expert on foreign policy and a regular contributor to several Arab and English newspapers. He is a member of the board of directors at the Damascus University Center for Strategic Studies and Research and Chief Editor of Syria Tribune, a newly established online English newspaper.

Bassma Kodmani is the Executive Director of the Arab Reform Initiative, a consortium of Arab policy research institutes working collaboratively on reforms and democratic transitions in the Arab world. She is also associate research fellow at the *Centre d'Études et de Recherché Internationals* (CERI) at Sciences-Po, and senior adviser of the *Académie Diplomatique Internationale* in Paris. From 1999 to 2005 she headed the Governance and International Cooperation program at the Ford Foundation office for the Middle East and North Africa, based in Cairo. Prior to moving to Cairo, she established and directed the Middle East Program at the *Institut Français des Relations Internationales* (IFRI) in Paris from 1981 to 1998 and was Associate Professor of International Relations at Paris University. She holds a PhD in Political Science from Sciences-Po in Paris. She has authored books and articles on conflicts in the Middle East, regional security, the Palestinian question, political developments in Arab societies and the relationship between religious and political authority in the Muslim world. Her latest book *Abattre les murs* (Breaking Walls) was published in France in February 2008.

David W. Lesch is Professor of Middle East History and Chair of the Department of History at Trinity University in San Antonio, Texas. He received his PhD in Middle East History from Harvard University. His most recent books are: *The Arab-Israeli Conflict: A History* (Oxford University Press, 2007); *The Middle East and the United States: A Historical and Political Reassessment* (Westview Press, 2007); and *The New Lion of Damascus: Bashar al-Asad and Modern Syria* (Yale University Press, 2005).

The St Andrews Papers on Modern Syrian Studies is published by the Centre for Syrian Studies, University of St Andrews, Scotland and distributed by Lynne Rienner Publishers, Boulder, CO, USA. The series remit is to publish cutting edge contemporary research and analysis on modern Syria, with the focus on the contemporary economic "transition" (reform) and on Syria's current security problems.
http://www.st-andrews.ac.uk/~wwwir/syrian/

We invite submission of unsolicited papers, particularly papers that report on current empirical research on Syria. Send paper submissions to series editor, Raymond Hinnebusch, School of International Relations, University of St Andrews, St Andrews, Fife, Scotland, KY15 7SP, U.K. or by e-mail to rh10@st-andrews.ac.uk.